Vital Aspects of African Linguistics

A Partial List of Linguistics Texts by the Press

1. *Four Decades in the Study of Languages & Linguistics in Nigeria*
2. *In the Linguistic Paradise*
3. *Languages & Culture in Nigeria*
4. *Globalization & the Study of Languages in Africa*
5. *Trends in the Study of Language & Linguistics in Nigeria*
6. *Convergence: English and Nigeria Languages*
7. *Language, Literature and Culture in Nigeria*
8. *Critical Issues in the Study of Linguistics, Languages & Literatures in Nigeria*
9. *Language Policy, Planning & Management in Nigeria*
10. *Language, Literature & Communication in a Dynamic World*
11. *Language, Literature & Culture in a Multilingual Society*
12. *Issues in Contemporary African Linguistics*
13. *Numeral Systems of Nigerian Languages*
14. *The Syntax of Igbo Causatives: A Minimalist Account*
15. *The Eleme Phonology*
16. *Basic Linguistics: For Nigerian Language Teachers*
17. *English Studies and National Development*
18. *Language, Literature & Literacy in a Developing Nation*
19. *Language & Economic Reforms in Nigeria*
20. *The Syntax & Semantics of Yorùbá Nominal Expressions*
21. *Functional Categories in Igbo*
22. *Affixation and Auxiliaries in Igbo*
23. *The Bette Ethnography: Theory & Practice*
24. *A Grammar of Contemporary Igbo*
25. *Language Endangerment: Globalisation and the Fate of Minority Languages*

VITAL ASPECTS OF AFRICAN LINGUISTICS

Okon Essien, *FMLAN, FNAL, FIIA, OON, JP*
Professor of Linguistics
Department of Linguistics & Nigerian Languages
University of Uyo, **Nigeria**

M & J Grand Orbit Communications Ltd., Port Harcourt

M & J Educational Books
No. 10 Nchia Street, Delta Park
Box 237 Uniport P.O., University of Port Harcourt, **Nigeria**
E-mail: mekuri01@yahoo.com   Phone: 08033410255

© 2016 Okon Essien

All rights reserved. No part of this work may be used or reproduced in any manner, by print, photoprint, microfilm, or any other means, without written permission from the Copyright owner except in the case of brief quotations embodied in critical articles and reviews.

ISBN 978-978-54164-4-2

Published by
M & J Grand Orbit Communications Ltd., Port Harcourt

Overseas Distributors:
African Books Collective
PO Box 721, Oxford OX1 9EN, United Kingdom
Tel: +44 (0) 1865 58 9756, Fax: +44 (0) 1865 412 341
US Tel: +1 415 644 5108
Customer Services please email
orders@africanbookscollective.com
For Warehouse/shipping/deliveries:
+44 (0) 1865 58 9756

Dedication

IN MEMORY OF

LATE MARIA OKON ESSIEN
A GEM OF A HOUSE WIFE

Acknowledgements

First, I would like to express my profound gratitude to the University of Uyo, in particular to the Vice-Chancellor, Professor Akaneren Essien, whose job offer made it possible for me to return to my land of birth and primary education after many years of sojourn. The circumstances of the writing of this volume are related in the introductory chapter.

Secondly, I would like to thank the following for commissioning me to write the works in the first instance, which now form the chapters of this book: The University of Calabar for the inaugural lecture (2003); Association of Nigerian Language Teachers (ANLAT) for the keynote paper (2005); the Nigerian Academy of Letters (NAL) for the Annual Lecture (2006), the Department of Linguistics and Nigerian Languages in collaboration with the Department of Classical and Vernacular Languages, University of Sao Paulo, Brazil for the Syntax-Phonology keynote address (2006), Dr. Marcia Santos Duarte de Oliveira, Department of Classical and Vernacular Languages, University Sao Paulo, Brazil for the African Linguistics Lecture (2007); and Professor Obot Antiabong, Registrar, National Post-Graduate Medical College of Nigeria, Lagos, for his invaluable assistance in Lagos before I left for Brazil. Without these bodies and the individuals, there would have been no papers to put together for this publication.

Thirdly, I am highly indebted to the following for their individual/corporate role that facilitated the publication of this book: Professor Ozo-mekuri Ndimele for the publication itself, Miss Blessing Robert of the Faculty of Science, University of Calabar and Alhaji M. Nya of the Department of Linguistics & Nigerian Languages, Uyo, for their computer expertise, Miss Mfon B. Udo, a graduate student of the Department of Linguistics & Nigerian Languages, Uyo, for her painstaking proof-reading, and the Chapel of Redemption for spiritual direction while I was in Calabar.

And lastly, but by no means the least, I am most grateful to my loving wife Eme, a gem of a house wife, and my dear children at home in Nigeria and abroad: Richard, Mabel, Imabong, Inemesit and Anthony for their ever caring and concerned attitude all the time. May God bless my wife and my children. And to God be the glory.

Okon Essien
University of Uyo

Table of Contents

Dedication   v
Acknowledgements   vi

Chapter 1   1
General Introduction   1
1.0 Preliminary remarks   1
1.1 Reasons for publishing this volume   2
1.2 The summaries   3
1.2.2 Nigerian languages and empowerment   5
1.2.3 Languages, literacy and nation building   5
1.2.4 Syntax-phonology interface in African languages   6
1.2.5 Introduction to African linguistics   7

Chapter 2   9
Language and Power   9
2.01 Preamble   9
2.02 Introduction   10
2.1 What is language?   11
2.2 What is linguistics?   18
2.2.1 Specialties in linguistics   20
2.2.2 The advent of linguistics in the University of Calabar   27
2.3 Definition of power   29
2.4 The power of language   30
2.4.1 As a verbal communicative means   30

2.4.1.2 Persuasion	32
2.4.1.3 Propaganda	34
2.5 Language and religion	40
2.6 Individual languages and power	41
2.6.1 Individual languages & their relative powers	44
2.7 Empowerment of powerless/weak Nigerian languages	49
2.7.1 How to empower such languages	50
2.8.0 Summary and conclusion	53
Chapter 3	55
Nigerian Languages and Empowerment	55
3.0 Preamble	55
3.1 Introduction	55
3.2 Definitions	55
3.2.1 Nigerian languages	55
3.2.1.2 Commonness in Nigerian languages	57
3.3 Nigerian languages & classification according to size	60
3.4 Empowerment	63
3.5 What has happened to language development projects?	66
3.6.0 Language as a mirror of the mind & culture	69
3.6.1 Language as a mirror of the mind	69
3.6.2 Language as a mirror of culture	70
3.7 Suggestions	71

Chapter 4	79
Syntax-Phonology Interface in African Languages	79
4.1 Introduction	79
4.2 Phonology & syntax	80
4.2.1 Phonology	80
4.2.2 Syntax	83
4.3 Phonology & syntax in African languages	84
4.4 Tone	85
4.4.1 Morpho-phonemic tone rule	87
4.5 Interaction of phonology & syntax in tense morphology	89
4.5.1 Preliminary remarks	89
4.6.0 Auxiliary focus or syntactic conditioning of tense?	93
4.7 Conclusion	100
Chapter 5	103
Language, Literacy and Nation Building	103
5.1 Introduction	103
5.2.1 Language & its attributes	103
5.2.2 The biology & power of language	109
5.2.3 Language is power	111
5.3 Literacy	112
5.3.1 Advantages of literacy	113
5.3.2 Literacy & micro-minor languages	117
5.3.3 Functional literacy	120
5.4 Nation building	122

Chapter 6	**129**
Introduction to African Linguistics	**129**
6.1 Introduction	129
6.2 Justification of African linguistics	131
6.3 The beginnings of African linguistics	132
6.4 The objective of the course	134
6.5 Structural characteristics of African languages	136
6.5.1 Phonology	136
6.5.1.1 Common phonemes/segmental units of African languages	136
6.5.1.1.1 Implosives	137
6.5.1.1.2 Labio-velar stops (or doubly articulated stops)	139
6.5.1.1.3 Initial nasal consonant clusters NC	141
6.5.1.1.4 Systems & vowel processes	146
6.5.1.1.4.1 Vowel harmony	148
6.5.1.2 Prosodic system & tone	151
6.5.1.2.1 Tonal phenomena	155
6.5.1.2.1.1 Downdrift & downstep	155
6.5.1.2.1.2 Downstep	156
6.5.1.3 Tone & intonation	158
6.6 Morphology & syntax	160
6.6.1 Language types	161
6.6.2 Ideophones	168
6.7 Syntax	173
6.7.1 Basic sentence units in simple sentences	174
6.7.1.1 Basic word order in simple sentences	176
6.7.1.2 Cross-referencing NPs with VPs	179

6.7.1.3 Commands & questions	180
6.7.1.4 Negation	182
6.7.1.5 Serial construction	184
6.7.1.6 Relative clauses	184
6.8 Pronominal systems	186
6.9 Some parts of speech systems	192
6.9.1 Adjectives	192
6.9.2 Adverbs	193
6.10 Verbal system	196
6.10.1 Inflection & types	197
6.10.2 Auxiliary focus or syntactic conditioning of tense allomorphs?	199
6.10.3 Verbal extensions	204
6.10.4 Argument structure of verbs	205
6.10.5 Stative and non-stative verbs	207
6.11 Classification of African languages	209
6.11.1 Greenberg's classification of African languages	212
6.11.1.1 Greenberg's analysis itself	214
6.12 Afroasiatic	219
6.12.1 A run-down of the Afroasiatic families	221
6.12.2 What evidence is there for Greenberg's Afroasiatic classification	225
6.12.3 Morphology	227
6.12.3.1 Personal pronouns	227
6.12.3.2 Case markers	228
6.12.3.3 Verbal morphemes	229
6.12.4 Word formation processes	230
6.13 Khosian	231

6.13.1 Post-Greenberg classification	234
6.14 Nilo-Saharan	241
6.15 Afrosiatic (AA)	242
6.16 Khosian	245
6.16.1 Typological & areal classifications of African languages	247
6.16.2 Typological classification	248
6.16.3 Subject/object	251
6.16.4 Subject/object indexation typology	252
6.16.5 Definiteness & referentiality	253
6.16.6 Number	254
6.16.7 Word order typology (syntax)	254
6.16.8 Types of verbal inflection	255
6.16.8 Serial verbs	256
References	259

Chapter 1
General Introduction

1.0 Preliminary remarks

This volume covers the period between 2003, when I was able to present my long awaited inaugural lecture, and 2007, when I was kindly invited by the Department of Linguistics, University of Sao Paulo, Brazil to visit it and to introduce African Linguistics. The scope of the volume is determined by the number of paper or lectures that I delivered as I was invited. For this reason there isn't much unity in the issues discussed other than my own distinctive approach to issues, if there is anything like that. The volume therefore contains the following rather unrelated issues – "Languages and Power" (my 2003 Inaugural lecture), "Nigerian Languages and Empowerment (a 2005 keynote paper), Syntax-Phonology Interface in African Languages" (a 2006 Keynote paper), "Language, Literacy and Nation Building (a NAL Annual Lecture), "Introduction to African Linguistics (a USP Lecture 2007). These are by no means the only papers commissioned and presented during the five years. Quite a few, like "Language and the Nigerian Reforms Agenda and "The so-called Downstepped Tone," have been published already elsewhere.

1.1 **Two reasons compelled me to publish this volume**
(i) Articles in learned Journals, though highly rated- probably more so than book publications in many universities in this country- are far less accessible to a wider audience than books,. Indeed the Faculty of Arts, to which I belong, is a Faculty of books and erudition. Because some of the papers contain weighty and challenging linguistic issues of national importance, I consider that such issues should be made available to as large an audience as possible in the nation we know and have, Nigeria.

The other reason is somewhat personal and some may even say arrogant. Each of the papers became its own writer somewhere along the line and finally concluded itself. At the end of the day, it often became clear to me that is was NOT I, Okon Essien, who was writing, but the Holy Spirit, to whom I always prayed for inspiration, guidance and leading.

Just consider this simple but effective definition of Language.

Put more simply, language is a system of rules and principles in which sound, structure and meaning are integrated for communication (cf. Language, Literacy and Nation Building).

Or this charming and conversation-like paragraph:

Language is both a cultural index and the expression of that index. When you are learning a language, you are entering the domain and terrain of the native speakers of the language. You get to understand the belief system, the taboos, the totems, the values, the ethos, the fears and hopes, the foods, the traditions, the clothes, the ceremonies, the names and the naming system and whatever identifies the people by way of their mental and creative outputs: religion, literature and the arts in general, economic well-being, education, technology etc. This is indeed an enormous power of language (cf. Nigerian Languages and Empowerment).

It is hoped that readers will find each contribution useful and intellectually stimulating. To be reader-friendly, the five contributions have been summarized, explicated and their significances stated or discussed. Some of the contributions have been updated in the light of comments by colleagues, new developments, new knowledge and new visions. It is hoped that all these have resulted in a much richer and more profound volume for the reader and to the glory of God.

1.2 The summaries

1.2.1 We begin with the inaugural lecture (2003). This is probably the most spiritually inspired academic work I have ever written. At the end of the lecture, I had an unusual sense of satisfaction that I had used my discipline to glory God. In this lecture, we have been able to raise quite a number of issues, the most important of which, to me, are:

(i) The divine origin and the biological basis of language, its definition and the discipline that studies it, and the concept of power, which underlies it;

(ii) Highlighted the various aspects of the powers of language;

(iii) Dispassionately but movingly highlighted the special problems of dispowered minor and micro-minor languages in Nigeria and suggested ways to empower them.

In conclusion, because language is an attribute of God- He who made us fearfully and wonderfully, also made us linguistically – we are indeed innately powerful verbally. Therefore, nothing should be done by any person, group, or authority wittingly or unwittingly to weaken or dispower anybody's or community's language, the vital highway between God and man.

1.2.2 Nigerian languages and empowerment

This paper is somewhat thematically related to the inaugural lecture because power (or lack of it) is central to it. In this paper, Nigerian languages, defined as "those indigenous or native languages spoken within the geo-political boundaries of the nation-state known as Nigeria derived etymologically from the River Niger, one of the great rivers of the country", is classified into four groups or categories according to numerical strength, i.e. number of speakers per each language, namely major, medium, minor and micro-minor. Power, from which empowerment is derived, is non-technically defined in this paper as "simply strength, might ability to compel some individual, authority, control, a right, dominance or domination. The paper then traces the history of government efforts to develop and empower some Nigerian languages, especially the major and some medium languages but is unimpressed, and maintains that as a mirror of the mind more needs to be done, and concludes with a number of far-reaching suggestions.

1.2.3 Language, literacy and nation building

In this paper, as in the other two papers, the notion of language as power is central. In it, we have demonstrated that no nation has been built without a written language and that literacy must create a truly educated citizenry, a clear conscience and freedom from corruption that stultifies a nation. The paper also examines literacy among micro-minor languages speakers, and offers suggestions.

1.2.4 Syntax-phonology interface in African languages

This is a core linguistic paper, marrying phonology and syntax in novel ways from the perspective of African languages. This is hardly surprising because from the early days of what is now described as classical generative phonology, pioneered by Noam Chomsky and Morris Halle (cf. Chomsky and Halle 1968), the phonology of a language has always been viewed as an integral part of grammar comprising the three major components of syntax, semantics and phonology. In African languages phonology and syntax directly relate to each other through tone. At the lexical level, tone co-operates with consonantal and vocalic segments to create meaning. At the grammatical level tone participates in grammatical processes phone-syntactically.

This paper also describes the interaction of phonology and syntax in tense phonology in African languages and compares it to the ± focus auxiliary treatment of this matter by Hyman and Watters (1984). The paper concludes that this is an important contribution of African languages to linguistics, a contribution which goes beyond the Hyman and Watters auxiliary focus and which Western analysts ought to consider seriously.

1.2.5 Introduction to African linguistics

This paper, commissioned by the Department of Linguistics, University of Sao Paulo for graduate students there (for whom African Linguistics is a novelty) is very comprehensive and African students will find it equally useful. It covers justification of African Linguistics, the beginnings of African Linguistics, objectives of the course, structural characteristics of African languages, genetic classification of African languages, typological and areal classifications, etc.

This is a special volume. The idea of putting all the papers together into a volume like this came to me when I began to unpack my things from the University of Calabar to arrange them together in my new environment. By sheer luck, I found the five papers, about which I had almost forgotten. Immediately an idea came to me "Why don't you put these papers together as a book publication". That's how the volume was conceived. To God be the glory.

Chapter 2
Language and Power

2.01 **Preamble**

> In the beginning was the Word
> And the Word was with God
> And the Word was God.
> He was with God in the beginning
> Through Him all things were made
> Without him nothing was made that was made
> (John 1:1-3) (KJV).

Mr. Chairman and Vice-Chancellor, this is at the very heart of my lecture this afternoon: the power of language, for God, the Father of Jesus Christ, the Word, brought form, order, discipline and beauty into our world, which was chaotic, by the power of the spoken word, as clearly and unequivocally demonstrated here:

> Now the earth was formless and empty,
> Darkness was over the surface of the deep
> And the spirit of God was hovering over the waters.
> And God Said, "Let there be Light,"
> And there was light (Gen. 1:2-3).

So God spoke and things happened by the power of His words. And since Jesus Christ, His one and only begotten

Son is the Word or the Good News, then by simple logic God spoke His Son and He, "being in very nature God," according to Philipians 2:6, became flesh, the second Adam, through the Virgin Mary, for our redemption.

So Jesus Christ is not only the Son of God but also His Word by which the world was created and through which all things have been and will be done. If the Word is also = language and the Word is power, then language is = power.

The relationship between power and word becomes even more exciting if we remember that words are not only spiritual – God spoke the world into existence – they are also physical, since sounds that make up a word or words are wave-like energies, as defined by physicists. And Jesus Christ is both flesh/blood and Spirit- indeed Emmanuel "God with us", (cf. Matthew 1:23[b])

If Christ is the Word, then He is the embodiment of language. Mr. Chairman, this is the source of the power of language. This is why I couldn't agree more with Lucan (1966) that "it is the world of words that creates the world of things," in so far as we believe that the words have a divine source. This divine source of language physically transmitted as wave – like energies is the basis of what we are going to say this afternoon.

2.02 Introduction

Mr. Chairman and Vice-Chancellor, in this Lecture, we propose to define language and power and critically examine the interface between them in society concluding with lessons and suggestions for us in this country with a multiplicity of languages, a majority of which are powerless. Naturally we will also define linguistics, mention some of its specialties and give a brief history and achievements of the Department.

2.1 What is language?

In a way, we all know what language is, for a vast majority of human beings know and use at least one language. Indeed that is why everyone thinks he/she is an authority in language and there are myriad definitions (or so called definitions) of language.

Although Robins (1979) does not think much of formal definitions of language because, according to him, they "tend to be trivial and uninformative," we believe inadequate as a definition may be, it does give at least one piece of information or a slice of truth. Many inadequate definitions, therefore, are likely to give many pieces of information for at least the layman. We shall, therefore, present a few definitions of language including our own preferred definition.

Sapir (1921:8), one of the two well-known American linguists who popularized the hypothesis of linguistic determinism and linguistic relatively, to which we shall return, defines language as, "purely human and non-instinctive method of communication of ideas, emotions and desires by voluntarily produced symbols." This is one of the most frequently quoted definitions especially by people outside the discipline of linguistics yet, as observed by Lyons (1981:3-4) "It suffers from several defects." For example, a lot more is communicated than just ideas, emotions, and desires. And this is why Essien (1983) has gone further to expound on it in this way:

> Language is the thing with which we can best imagine, create, aspire, desire, feel and express our soul, enlarge our mental horizon and fulfill all that man is capable of.

Secondly, it does not say what kind of symbols are voluntarily produced - light, electromagnetic, sound, etc. Even voluntariness is open to question because there is much else that is voluntarily and non-instinctively produced that we do not normally count as language that we all know and use. This includes gestures, postures, eye-gaze, whistling, etc (cf. Lyons 1981:3). Nor does it mention a very essential aspect of language, which Bloch and Trager (1942:5) do, namely, the relationship between the words of a language and their meaning.

However, it does include two essential aspects, namely: It is limited to the human race, the homo-sapiens and it is used for communication, however inadequately communication is viewed. In addition, no matter how much linguists disagree among themselves, the human language is infinitely and qualitatively less instinctive than animal communication systems.

A second popularly quoted definition – which I first heard myself in the 1960s as an undergraduate – is Bloch and Trager's (1942:5) Bloch and Trager define language as, "a system of arbitrary vocal symbols by means of which a social group co-operate." Again I begin by explaining what is wrong with this definition. I'm intrigued by the expression *social group*. What does it really mean? For a social group refers to the vertical structure of the society – the upper (moneyed) class, the middle class, the working class, etc., considering a highly stratified society like the United Kingdom. Does it mean that language is used in only intra-class or group communication? As far as it is known linguistically, language is rotted in a community or society. From this point of view, we have various linguistic (or speech) communities such as Hausa, Igbo, Yoruba, Ibibio, Efik, Eggon, etc., communities. Within these communities, however, we do have social groups or classes which speak variations of the same language characterizing their respective community. I am surprised that Sir John Lyon's (and Sir John was my lecturer in Edinburgh) criticism of Bloch and Trager's definition of language, which follows, did not see anything wrong with a definition of language which sees it from the narrow point of view of a social group, rather than from an entire community view point. Sir John's criticism is repeated below:

> What is striking about this definition [that is Bloch and Trager's] in contrast with Sapir's, is that it makes no appeal, except indirectly and by implication, to the communicative function of

language. Instead, it puts all the emphasis upon its social function and, in so doing, it takes a rather narrow view of the role that language plays in society.

However, the definition advances Sapir's voluntarily produced symbols by stating that such symbols are vocalic, i.e. sound, for there is no word without a sound (or sounds). We return to this when we come to our own definition.

Noam Chomsky, the greatest and most influential linguist of our time, defines language in this way: "From now on I will consider a language to be a set (finite or infinite) of sentences, each finite in length and constructed out of a finite set of elements." This purely structural definition of language "says nothing about the communicative function of a natural or non natural language; it says nothing about the symbolic nature of elements or sequences of them," as rightly observed by Sir John Lyons (1981:7). I can only say here that Chomsky is too intelligent to say simply what language is for the non-initiate.

In 1968, Chomsky together with Halle gave a better definition (of Language) as follows:

> We may think of a language as a set of sentences, each with an ideal phonetic form and an associated intrinsic and semantic interpretation.

Although this definition includes a very important aspect of language, the sound or vocal aspect, it is still silent on the nature of the relationship between sound and meaning as well as on the communicative function of language.

Before I define language in my own way, let me amuse you with this ideologically feminist definition by Cameron (1990).

> Languages are cultural edifices whose norms are laid down in things like grammars, stylebooks and other glossaries – all of which have historically been compiled by men, and conservative men at that.

Male chauvinists, please hold on before you crucify Cameron. We don't have to go too far to illustrate the point of this definition, namely, that language is male-made. Or can you explain why Ibibio has a word primarily for a female prostitute – akpara – but none for a male one (cf. Okon and Akpan 2001) and yet Ibibio men, like all men globally, are far more promiscuous than women. It does appear that as far as Ibibio men are concerned, a man does not prostitute and therefore there is no need for a word for a concept that does not exist. Isn't this also true of men of other ethnic groups? Even from English the dictionary definition of prostitute given by Cambridge International Dictionary of English below:

"Prostitute: a person, usually a woman, who has sex with someone else for money" somewhat vindicates Cameron.

After that comic relief, let me define language as I see it. This definition following several earlier definitions is my 2003 definition so far (cf. 2003[b]).

> Language is a system of structural arbitrary vocal symbols by means of which human beings make meaning and communicate and interact with each other in a given community. Put more simply, language is a system of rules and principles in which sound, structure and meaning are integrated for communication.

We explain a few key terms here. As a system, the components of language are ordered, not haphazard. Language is primarily vocal or spoken, as we have already said in the preamble, but the sounds which it comprises, must correspond to meaning, otherwise we would be making just noises, instead of talking language. This implies that our utterances must also be appropriate to the situation, otherwise communication breaks down. But the relationship between the sounds of a language and what they mean or refer to in our real world is, for the most part, arbitrary. There is no logical or compelling reason, for example, why the sequence of sounds [e], [g], and [o] with a particular tonal melody (high-down stepped high) in the Igbo word *'ego'* 'money' should refer to that object which we all so badly need, any more than the English people have a reason for calling what the Igbo call **ego** money. Sounds and their sequences in words, phrases and sentences simply arbitrarily refer to what they refer to or mean in individual languages by convention. Of course there are onomatopoeic words and ideophones whose meanings seem to be related to, or can be determined by the sounds. Onomatopoeic words include examples such as **bang, click,** etc., in English, the ideophones include words such as **jim** in a number of our languages for the sound a heavy object falling and in the indeterminate lengthening of a final vowel or nasal to indicate duration, distance or quality as in the following examples in Ibibio:

(1)   a. Ńda-a-a-a   'I waited, I waited, I waited'
       b. Áyàiyá-a-a-a   'So very very pretty'

By and large, however onomatopoeic and ideophonic words are very few in any language.

Philosophically, language has been described by Chomsky (1968) as "a species-specific human possession, the human essence, the quality of mind that are, as far we know, peculiar to man" and Essien (1990:168) as "the quintessence of man's humanity." It is our earnest hope that a proper understanding of this "human essence," this "quintessence of man's humanity," this defining attribute of man will enhance our understanding of ourselves as homo-sapiens.

Before we turn to the next section, may we emphasize that language communication must be viewed in all its ramifications, for we use language not only positively to teach, explain, inform, direct, enlighten, praise, pray, please, etc. but also negatively to cheat, deceive, lie, mislead, misinform, misdirect, deride, insult, antagonize, etc.

2.2 What is linguistics?

Perhaps I should begin as I commonly do when asked to explain what linguistics is, or how many languages I speak as a linguist, by explaining first of all what it is not so as to disabuse the mind of the layman. Linguistics is not the learning or studying of many languages for the sole purpose of being able to speak, read or write them, although knowledge of many languages would obviously be of advantage to the linguist, as a scientist. Nor is the linguist one who speaks many languages. You may refer to such a talented person as a polyglot, which I wish I were.

Linguistics is the scientific study of language as an entity or phenomenon through objective and rigorous analysis. It is a science because work on language is done, according to Sir John Lyons (1968), by means of controlled and empirically verifiable observations and with reference to some general theory of language structure.

For the chemist, elements and their combinations and reactions constitute his domain of investigation and study, for the physicist, it is matter and energy, while for the biologist it is living things (or physical life itself). For the linguist, then, language is his/her field and he/she approaches it with the same neutrality, the same rigour, the same exhaustiveness that characterize the physical sciences. Indeed linguistics is frequently referred to as a linguistic science. It is not surprising, therefore, that Carroll (1953) describes it as "the most advanced of all social sciences with close resemblance to physics and chemistry. In even more flattering terms Levi-Strauss (1953:250:251) has compared the discovery that language consists of phonemes and morphemes to the Newtonian revolution in physics.

In the best tradition of science, quite often linguists from different countries (and even continents) working independently on totally different language data come to the same or similar conclusions. A classic case of relevance involves a certain linguistic phenomenon in Hausa and Ibibio, two very different languages genetically. For some years now one Professor Zima of the Institute of Theoretical Studies, Charles University, Prague, the Czech Republic and I have been working and unknown to each other on Hausa and Ibibio, respectively. However, through our individual international publications, we have discovered that our independent analyses of our data in Hausa and Ibibio respectively have come to the same conclusion revealing one theoretical insight. In a personal letter to me from Prague, he said:

> I am glad you have found my papers and reviews so useful. In fact our common work is a classic

example of how two linguists approaching the same or similar problems from different platforms may independently confirm their achievements and results.

If this is not a manifestation of science, Mr. Vice-Chancellor, I don't know what else is.

2.2.1 Specialties in linguistics

On the one hand, linguistics can be divided into two broad specialties, theoretical linguistics and applied linguistics with the former primarily concerned with the theory of language structure, and the latter with the applications of linguistic findings to practical situations. One very important area of linguistic application is to language teaching. There is no way one can be a good teacher of English (or any other language for that matter) without knowledge of the discipline of linguistics (other things being equal), anymore than there can be a good medical doctor without knowledge of the physiology and anatomy of the human body. This is no longer a debate in the developed world. Yet today in this country all kinds of people, geographers, historians, economists, science graduates, etc teach English in our schools without any knowledge of linguistics at all. All these are quack English teachers! Any wonder that the standard of English usage is so appallingly low.

On the other hand, there is a dichotomy between synchronic and historical/diachronic linguistics. The former is concerned with language as it is spoken and used today. Synchronic Efik or Ejagham is Efik or Ejagham spoken and used today. Historical/Diachronic linguistics is concerned with the study of languages over varying periods of time, or relationships (or otherwise) among the various languages of the world in various countries and their regions or sections (e.g. Nigeria and its states and geographical regions like Eastern Nigeria, geographical regions like Southern Africa, sub-continents like India and continents like Europe). According to Williamson (1988.4),

> One of the tenets of historical linguistics [is] that present day languages are the varied developments or continuations of an older, original language, or proto-language. A proto-language, like any other language, differentiates into dialects and these dialects, if left to themselves, gradually develop into independent languages; but so long as some original similarities between such daughter languages remain... they serve to trace the original notion that languages belong to families, each family descending from a common ancestor or proto-language.

Linguistically, or better still, genealogically, four, major families of languages are represented in Nigeria: Chadic, to which Hausa belongs, Nilo-Saharan, to which Kanuri belongs, Semitic, to which Shuwa Arab spoken in Borno State belongs, and the last, and by far the largest, the

Niger-Congo, to which all Southern and most Northern Nigerian languages belong. If languages that are genealogically (or genetically) related are traceable to one parent or proto-language, then most of us in this country are at least distant cousins. When we war against each other, as we once did- and are doing now and then in the name of ethnic or state origin- may we never blame it on our languages: the fault, dear fellow Nigerians is not in our languages, but in ourselves, our greed, our acquisitive instincts and our selfishness (cf. Essien 2000a).

Other areas of linguistics include the following:

a) **Psycholinguistics**

Every language has its own grammar. This grammar, technically referred to as competence, is mentally represented as a system of rules and principles acquired, or to use a more technical term, internalized in the way we shall discuss in development linguistics below. How this mentally represented grammar is employed in the production and comprehension of speech, a manifestation of language, is the subject matter of psycholinguistics. However, in a more general sense, psycholinguistics is defined as the study of language and mind. We generally hear distinctly and understand those we like, love, respect and admire and those we do not, we also do not understand.

In recent years, language acquisition, which used to come under psycholinguistics, is now commonly treated under what is known as developmental linguistics. For the benefit of this wonderful audience, I'm going to say a little more about this area. How do we acquire language? By inheritance in much the same way we inherit height, intelligence, colour of the skin, texture of the hair, or temper? The answer is obviously no, for an Agwagune child born of two Agwagune parents will speak no word of Agwagune if, at the critical stage of language acquisition this child is not exposed to that language, but rather to some other language (or languages) like Chinese or German. Yet inheritance of a sort is involved in language acquisition, as we shall see presently.

By habit formation, as we form smoking, drinking, siesta, etc. habits? Language acquisition is far from being habitual in the sense of being accustomed to doing something like praying every morning and every evening.

(b) **Developmental linguistics**

How do we acquire language then? Language acquisition takes place in childhood between the ages of one and six maturing fully by ten. Chomsky (1981) and Lenneberg (1967) from the standpoint of a mentally representable grammar and psychology and the biology of the brain have postulated a biological basis for language acquisition insisting that there is an innate faculty of language or what Radford *et al.* (1999) call acquisition programme in the brain making language acquisition and use possible. This, it is maintained emphatically, is specific to human beings but unavailable to any non-human animal including the most intelligent chimpanzee ever found on the face of the earth.

Chomsky, in particular, has progressed from characterizing this innate endowment as incorporating a language Acquisition Device (LAD) in the 1960's to Universal Grammar (or principles of UG) in recent times.

Perhaps a brief description of the innate faculty of language is necessary at this point. This is not to imply that the direct study of the human brain is by any means easy. Biologists, anatomists and physiologists acknowledge that the brain is very complex. This brief summary paraphrased from Radford et al (1999:2) suffices for our purposes.

The brain consists of several 'layers'. The layer which has evolved recently most characteristic of the higher primates like man is the cerebral cortex, which is the folded surface of the cerebral hemisphere. These contain grey matter, the home of the higher intellectual functions including language. The cerebral cortex can be damaged in a number of ways. For example, it may suffer an injury from a blow to the head. On the other hand, it may suffer internal damage owing to disease or a blockage in a blood vessel resulting in disruption of the blood supply and death of cortical cells. Areas of damage are generally referred to as lesions.

The study of patients with various types of brain damage has revealed that different parts of the brain are associated with different functions. Some of these functions include problem solving, motor control, auditory processing. A large disorder resulting from the brain is referred to as aphasia.

(c) Neurolinguistics

Curiously more light into the biological basis of language is coming strongly from the study of language disorders in neurolinguistics, the study of how linguistics knowledge is represented in the brain, as hypothesized above. If damage to a particular area of the brain results in a language disorder like complete language disorder or global aphasia, then we may suppose that there is an area for language in the brain. Aphasia, of course, occurs in varying degrees.

A language disorder can be genetic, i.e. internal, not caused by an external force. This referred to as specific Language Impairment (SLI), a specific type of which causes children not to properly absorb sounds and turn them into meaningful sentences (cf. Christie 1999:5), which is what language is all about. This group of genetico-linguistically (if I may be allowed to coin that expression) impaired patients "provides us with the chance of studying the effects of what is probably a genetically determined deficit on acquisition of language. The specificity of SLI is indicated by the fact that SLI subjects have normal non-verbal IQS, no hearing deficits and no obvious emotional or behavior difficulties", according to Christie.

Christie then goes on to conclude that SLI has a genetic source suggested by the fact:

> That it occurs in families... more frequent in boys than in girls and it affects both members of a pair of identical twins.

A genetic basis of language is also suggested in a research report by one Professor Jonathan Seekle, a professor of Molecular Medicine, who says, according to Christie (ibid):

> One study with an extended family in the United States has identified a single gene which seems to be important in the acquisition of language. Another study conducted among 3,000 twins concluded that 73% of variation in speech and language has a genetic basis. He says that may be an exaggeration but adds: even if it is only half, it tells you that there is a lot of genetic input into the development of language.

Could it be the language gene then that is responsible for why my own sister, Mrs. Grace Mendie and my own daughter, Mrs. Mabel Henderson, sound so alike in speaking that were they to be locked up in a room, one could hardly distinguish one from the other? Perhaps some of you in the audience may have similar cases.

You might have been wondering when I became a clinician. The fact of the matter is that language involves and affects the entire human spectrum. In any case since the language faculty is located in the brain-in the left hemisphere in most right-handed people-as widely reported by neurologists and neuro-surgeons, we might as well have a 'we' (if you will pardon my Scottish English here) taste of the structure of the human brain. In any case Mr. Chairman, isn't it high time that we established an institute of speech pathology, where neuro-surgeons, speech pathologists, neurolinguists and descriptive linguists could work together for the benefit of the linguistically impaired or disordered children of this country who number in millions?

2.2.2 The advent of linguistics at the University of Calabar

Mr. Chairman, kindly permit me to tell a small story. In 1976, the University of Calabar advertised for various vacant positions to be filled in what we called "Department of Linguistics and Nigerian Languages."

A young man from the Kano campus (now known as Bayero University) of Ahmadu Bello University applied for one of these positions and was offered a job. To his utter disappointment, he discovered that there was in fact no Department of Linguistics and Nigerian Languages. Rather he was being posted to the Department of English to teach English, a discipline for which he had no aptitude, even though academically and professionally he was qualified to be there. But he loved the discipline of linguistics Science better, a discipline in which he obtained his M.A. and Ph.D from two distinguished universities on both sides of the Atlantic. So he wasted no time and went straight to the then Vice-Chancellor, Professor Emmanuel Ayandele to complain. Professor Ayandele listened to him sympathetically, difficult as he appeared to some other people. The result was the immediate introduction of Linguistics beginning in 1977 and the young man became the only staff of the discipline with only four students, who transferred from the Department of English.

By the grace of God, today the smallest number of students in any one class in 70 and the Department has graduated many outstanding men and women for various walks of life, including NDLEA. Currently it is running BA, MA and PhD programmes and by the grace of God communication will be introduced. That indeed will be the logical conclusion, for there can be no proper definition of language without communication and the business of linguistics is language.

For the twenty-six years Linguistics has been here, it has made its impact nationally and internationally with the works of it staff being appreciated, not just in the US, the United Kingdom, Canada but also in Germany, Eastern Europe, Japan and Australia. In particular, linguistics in Calabar has **challenged successfully** and changed some obnoxious provisions of the national policy on language. But perhaps the greatest beneficiaries of Linguistics in Calabar are the Ibibio people of Akwa Ibom, whose language is now numbered among the 200 greatest in the world. Incidentally, Mr. Chairman, the 1976 young man is your inaugural lecturer.

Summarizing so far, we have examined some widely differing definitions of language and defined linguistics as a discipline, examined some of its branches, in particular developmental linguistics, which is concerned with language development or acquisition in children and traced the history of the department. In addition, we have given some of the achievements and contributions of the Department.

2.3 **Definition of power**

Unlike some of the definitions of language given in 2.1, the definitions of power are likely to be less technical in the sense that the term power is used and known outside a narrow professional circle. Power is used and known in everyday life and most of us (if not all) know what it is. That notwithstanding, we shall at least attempt to explain what power is. Power is strength, might, ability to compel some individual or institution to do what he/it would not like to do, authority, control, a right, dominance or domination. Power can be political, military (we have been through this in the last thirty years), educational, cultural, physical, social, sexual, religious, spiritual, etc. to mention the most obvious. In this lecture, however, power is viewed along a continuum from weak to strong, or from strong to the strongest. A weak entity is tautologically a non- strong entity. Put in another way, we view power as a coin with two sides: weak and strong. Power can also be used positively or negatively, regardless of the sphere. In language we have already indicated this in 2:1, drawing attention to the positive and negative communicative functions of language.

2.4 The power of language
2.4.1 As a verbal communicative means

Languages, as we have said earlier on (cf. 2.1) is a cognitive system, biologically represented in the brain or mind. Since as we know, the brain is the centre of man himself, or the centre of what is distinctively human, as some would say, then language, the very essence of man's humanity, is as essential and powerful as the very source of it, the brain.

It is language housed in the brain of man, which provides man the capacity of not only for conceptualizing the world about himself but also for naming or tagging every concept in the universe, a job which was assigned to Adam, according to Genesis 2:19-20, by God, thus making Adam the first ever linguist on earth (cf. Essien 2003a:2). This is a power or ability of enormous or stupendous proportion. Can anyone imagine a world of no language? For remember whether you are dreaming, praying or reading even silently, or writing or thinking, you are doing so in a language. Language is imminent in all of us who have acquired it until we die when language departs from the soul. No wonder Publius Syrus, according to Fry (1977) says: "Speech is a mirror of the soul: as a man speaks, so is he". So that is the power of language; provides man the capacity for conceptualizing the world and naming his mental concepts, and is his soul. In this way language rules the world.

And this leads me to an important aspect of conceptualization: thinking. Thinking is a mental activity and naturally related to language. People think in a language. It is arguable whether there can be any serious thinking or thought without language. Indeed what is commonly referred to as the Sapir-Whorf hypothesis not only emphasizes the primacy of language over thought but also linguistic determinism, which hypothesizes that individual languages determine the thinking pattern of its speakers. For example, according to this hypothesis, the English think the way they do because of English and similarly the Urhobo people think as they do because of the Urhobo language. Although this hypothesis has been debated upon and severely criticized in some cases by people who reject linguistic determinism or relativity – I am one of them – there is little doubt that the language one speaks influences, though it does not determine, one's thought. If language then is a medium of thought in any language community, then that is an awesome power of language.

Sometimes a word is not just a word: It may be a way of life, as **apartheid** in the South Africa of Pre-Mandela/cum ANC control by which one of the most oppressive and incredibly inhuman practices was perpetuated on fellow human beings simply because of the colour of the skin. Or it may carry an attitude like the Ibibio word **Utom:** 'work/job', But among the Ibibio, **utom** is not just work, it is something to be taken seriously. Thus there is a saying: **Anam nte utom**: 'he/she does something (understood by the hearer/listener) as seriously as work/job. Similarly among the Igbo, 'oji' is not just kola nut (or name of a person) but according to Achebe's ***Things Fall Apart*** "he who brings kola nut brings peace". We can go on and on.

The thing about words is that they not only have ordinary denotations (i.e. ordinary workaday meanings) but also associations, as literary critics know. These may be pleasant, unpleasant, frightening, awful or awesome, negative or positive, nauseating, revolting, conciliatory, offensive, etc. Each time we talk, we are emitting not only information, facts, figures, or arguments but wittingly or unwittingly, we are conveying our emotions, attitudes, fears, prejudices and aspirations among a whole range of indices. Naturally each of these indices carriers its own power or effect on the hearer/listener or audience.

I cannot leave this aspect of the power of language without considering persuasion and propaganda, for these are weapons that either win or wound.

2.4.1.2 Persuasion

This is a process by which someone tries, usually by reasoned arguments, logic, appeal to sound judgement, verbal finesse or artistry to win someone (or even himself/herself) to a particular point of view or programme at home, workplace, school, church, mosque, the market place in short whenever there is an audience. Parents persuade their children to do or not to do one thing or another. In the workplace, it is not always a matter of order from above. In the market place, the vendor tries to persuade his/her customer to buy his/her goods. Arguments arise now and then even in the military. A particular course is sometimes argued for. Even in Church, it is not always just God's truth that is given and therefore the parishioner is either to take or leave it. Who could ever beat St. Paul, let alone Jesus Christ Himself in argumentation? All pastors or evangelists know they have to use portions of the Bible situated in normal everyday life to persuade their audiences and win people for Christ.

Persuasions are, therefore, usually our normal or unmarked, to use a rather technical term in linguistics, and harmless mode of communication. Yet in this seeming harmlessness lies the power to get things done or undone. Very often where brutal or naked force fails, the power of words succeeds (cf. Okon 2003). Any wonder that it is often said that the pen is mightier than the sword. There is no modern war which has been fought and won without the power of words. Sometimes the mightier one of the warring nations is also the mightier by their own verbal weaponry. We shall return to this when we consider propaganda. But I would like to end this subsection by saying that physical or brute force merely compels silencing the inner man or soul (often only temporarily) without persuasion. Persuasion is one of language's finest and most potent weapons. In this regard, need I remind us that the applications, the memos, the contracts tenders, etc that succeed are usually the best-worded and most persuasive, except where the Nigerian factors come in.

2.4.1.3 Propaganda

We view propaganda as a programmed approach to winning one to one's point of view, side, idea, belief or creed by means of organized publicity. Unlike persuasion, it is unfortunately the misuse of the malleable property of language. These are some of the features of propaganda.

a. Polemic and invective-ridden;

b. Shows little or no scruples in using half-truths, exaggeration or even downright lies to achieve its objectives;

c. Commonly presents one position, view, hypothesis or approach as infallible or unassailable, and

d. Uses manipulative and emotive language.

These features singly or together can be lethal in the hands of irresponsible individuals, especially despots, a group of individuals or even governments. Consider one example of a propaganda material on the language policy of the former Soviet Union:

> In full conformity with the Constitution the equality of all languages is noted in the Program of CPSU... to continue promoting the free development of the languages of the people of the USSR to speak, and to bring up and educate their children, in any

language ruling out all privileges, restrictions or compulsions in the use of this or that language (Isayev 1977:20).

Observe the almost hyperbolic language of the author *promoting the free development of the languages of the USSR, to bring up and educate their children in any language ruling out all privileges, restrictions and compulsions, equality of all languages.*

Brave new ideas couched in brave new words on the surface. But in fact these were idealistic, for in practice the Soviets subtly coerced the non-Russian Soviets to learn and acquire Russian for whom Russian was described euphemistically as a second native language, as evidenced in the following:

> Clearly not all nations and people of the USSR are equally fluent in the Russian language as a second language. It is among the numerous peoples that enter into the Russian Federation that this language is most widely used. It is they who most frequently use the term second native language in relation to the Russian language, and there are grounds for objecting to this (Isayev 1977).

If non-Russians desire to speak Russian as "a second native language, "as the quotation above shows, the assertion that all languages in the Union are equal is hypocritical.

Indeed the following shows that wittingly or unwittingly, the Russian language played a central role in Soviet affairs:

> A concise definition of the place and role of the language of communication between the Soviet nations was formulated at the 22nd Congress of the CPSU: "The voluntary study of Russian in addition to the native language is of positive significance, since it facilitates reciprocal exchanges of experience and access of every nation and nationality to the cultural gains of all the other people of the USSR, and to the world culture. The Russian language has, in effect, become the common medium of intercourse of the USSR (Isayev 1977:335).

This is precisely the double- talk of the language propaganda. For the Soviets, the use of Russian all over the Soviet Empire was 'Voluntary' and "a distinguishing feature of the feudal and especially bourgeois states in the imposing on the other peoples of the language of the ruling people" (Isayev 1977:326).

It is not only the communists who used propaganda. The Western Capitalists, of course, did. Radio Free Europe, which broadcast propaganda materials daily in the various native languages of Eastern Europe, must have gone a long way to destabilize the Soviet Union and to cause its eventual collapse. Today capitalism is viewed in the West as the norm and any other form of economy cum political system-socialism, not to mention communism - is unusual, strange, outlandish, etc. - indeed marked, as we would say in linguistics. For most regular politicians in this country, Nigeria does not need an ideology. Yet clearly capitalism is simply an ideology. But it is so much a part of our polity that it has lost the 'danger' of an ideology.

When nations are not at war with each other, propaganda becomes a common tool often couched in the euphemism of 'the diplomatic war'. Even though Israel is by far militarily stronger than Arafat's Palestine, Israel still fights at the diplomatic level using and manipulating language to present its case before the international community. For the Israelis, the Palestinians are the terrorists. On the other hand, the Palestinians refer to their people as freedom fighters, suicide bombers as martyrs, while the Israelis are labeled Zionists and extremists seeking to exterminate them for their land.

Or consider the American spy plane detained by China not too long ago. The release of the pilot, the crew and other spy agents hinged on satisfactory language-apology, which the Americans abhorred preferring the world regret, which was rejected by the Chinese since regret doesn't imply responsibility for what happened-the death of a Chinese pilot. The Chinese insisted on the world *sorry* since that word implies responsibility and they got it and language won where military threat couldn't.

So clearly with language you can win or lose, you can inflame or sooth, you can live or die. The solution to delicate situations at all levels-village, ward, LGA, State, regional, national or international often comes not by physical or military might but by linguistic ingenuity, creativity, finesse and decorum.

Before we turn to the next section let me reiterate the powers of words. They can be vitriolic, inciting, offensive, insolent, provocative, destructive, etc. When released, they can be as incendiary as volcanoes or bombs and as penetratingly destructive as missiles. Many wars are known to have been fought, marriages broken, friendships torn apart and families in disarray because of the tongue.

In the Holy Bible, as reported in the Acts of the Apostles, the audience unwittingly caused an instant death of a Herod, when it said, after Herod's address. "This is the voice of a god, not of a man." Words can be like dangerous pets such as lions and pythons, which can turn even on their owners, when disturbed. And once uttered, harm can be done beyond repairs.

The Book of Proverbs, more than any books I have read, highlights profound insights into the power of language. Consider just a few of the enduring truths of language collaborating what we have said in this section:

(a) Reckless worlds pierce like a sword, but the tongue of the wise brings healing (Proverb 12:18).

(b) He who guards his lips guards his life but he who speaks rashly will come to ruin (Proverb 13:3)

(c) The tongue has the power of life and death (Proverbs 18:21[a]). Hasn't this proverb said it all? It is specially pertinent to husbands and wives, people about to get married, preachers, and medical doctors and nurses.

(d) Pleasant words are as an honey comb sweet to the soul and healing to the bones (Proverb 16:24)

And talking about doctors, Mr. Chairman, kindly permit me to tell another story which I read in one of the national dailies sometime ago in the 1980s. A ward round of doctors went like this verbally (reconstructed): "Good morning, doctor", said a nurse to a doctor. "Good morning, nurse," the doctor, replied. "How's this patient this morning?" asked the doctor. "He's for Coffin," the nurse replied. Immediately the doctor and the nurse rushed to the patient, who had almost developed a heart attack at the mention of coffin. "Phone Dr. Coffin please," requested the doctor, at which point the patient realized that Coffin was the name of a new doctor to treat him. Perhaps there should be no Dr. Mkpa (Dr. Death) or Dr. Udi (Grave) in our hospitals in this part of Nigeria. Should there be one, perhaps before patients, his/her professional tile should not be omitted. But a small incident such as this shows the delicate nature of the thing we so much take for granted: language. Need I caution on some of the rude and emotionally – charged memos/ letters we write to colleagues and authorities now and then? They hurt, they hurt.

2.5 Language and religion

If propaganda exploits the negative side of language, in religion we experience the spiritual power of speech. Religion is concerned with man's relationship to a supernatural being or power in the great drama of existence. Such a being is referred to as God in as many languages as human beings speak. Thus we have Ab*as*i, Chi*ne*ke, Ogun, Allah, etc. There are many kinds of religion in the world, the oldest of which is traditional religion, a religion in which people worship various deities and do homage to them. Other religions are Buddhism, Judaism, Hinduism, Shinotoism, Christianity, Islam, etc. Christianity, to which I subscribe, is said to be five centuries younger than Buddhism (cf. Isayev 1977: 30-31), having been born in AD I with the birth of the author and finisher of the faith, Jesus Christ. Islam followed in the 7th Century AD.

One strand runs through all religions- the adherents, worshippers or devotees have never seen their God but in faith they believe that God does exist. Language therefore becomes the most important means by which God's faithful people can communicate, fellowship or commune with Him. From the libation of the traditional worshipper to the Psalms, the Lord's Prayer, the Apostle's Creed, not to mention all the books of the Bible and the Koran, words and words are the medium. It is said in Christianity that prayer governs God and don't we pray in a language, whether Pharisee – like in the open or silently in our hearts? And as if to show the special power of God, as we saw in the Preamble, God created the universe by word. Is it any wonder then that in Christianity Jesus Christ is the word incarnate as Paul says in Romans 1:16:

> I am not ashamed of the gospel because it is the **power of God** for the salvation of everyone who believes, first for the Jews and then for the Gentiles.

This is the mystical power of language and the glory of man who is mysteriously and wonderfully made in the image and likeness of God. Man is God – like because, he like God, has language, unlike all other creation below him, which provides a highway between him and God.

Because God knew in advance that language would provide a highway between Him and man, God created the language faculty as part of man's biological or genetic make up (cf. 2.2.16). You may recall we said that man is born endowed with Universal Grammar (UG) or a set of UG principles, which are incorporated in the language faculty. This UG, then, enables the normal child to acquire any language to which he/she is exposed during the critical years of language acquisition.

In this way, the spiritual and the physical-actually the biological- are intertwined and man is what he is. Language is therefore, at once spiritual, physical, social and cultural; hence, its enormous powers and possibilities.

2.6 Individual languages and power

So far we have been looking at the powers of language in general as man's gift from God. In this section and the following ones, we will examine languages in competition, so to say, in human communities of varying sizes and complexities (e.g. LGAs, states in a federal set up such as Nigeria, regions of countries and continents, nation states and the international community).

A community may have just one speech form or language (though such communities, especially nations are very very few). Such a community is said to be monolingual and usually there is little or no linguistic conflict or clash of interest. Where the language of the community is socially differentiated there may be a problem, especially where the differences are correlated with status arising from education, wealth, royalty or political dominance. Such a social variant or dialect may assume importance or status that invests it with dominance. We shall return to the notion of dominance later.

It is in bilingual (i.e. speaking two languages) and multilingual (speaking many languages) communities such as nation states that the linguistic clash is often clear and sometimes even vicious, as in most African nations south of Sahara.

Because European nations knew the powers and potentials of language, multilingual European nations often respected linguistic sensitivities. Essien (forthcoming) has discussed the management of multilingualism in Europe.

One way Europe has been able to manage its multilingualism without sacrificing too much the principle of what has come to be known as language rights has come through national independence granted to some local ethnic minorities. Deutsche (1968), according to Wardhangh (1986:335), has documented the tremendous increase within Europe during the last 1000 years (counting from 1968 backwards) of what he calls "full-fledged" languages. In AD 950, there were only six such languages: Latin, Greek, Hebrew, Arabic, Old English and Church Slavonic. Over the years, this number has increased as European ethnic minorities or nationalities became fully independent, so that by 1937, there were 53 "full-fledged" official national languages. The number has obviously increased since 1937 such that what used to be ethnic languages like Czech and Slovak, are now "full-fledged" national languages.

As each new nation was born, a new national and official language was also born. Such a language (or languages) became basic expression of the identity and aspiration of the people and government. Governments of such new nations responded by embarking on language planning, that is "... government authorized long-term sustained and conscious efforts to alter a language," according to Weistein (1980:56). So it is quite clear from this that in those new nations of Europe, economic, legal, socio-cultural and linguistic developments, ingredients that are crucial in national development, were integrated. The new nations followed the foot-path of the older nations like France, Britain, Italy, Germany, Russia, etc. No wonder, then, European nations, old or new, are where they are – far above Black nations of Africa, south of the Sahara, whose development does not take cognizance of the enormous potentials and power of language. When Allen (1976) says that he who controls language controls history, he is partially right. But I would like to say that he who controls language controls history, power and destiny.

2.6.1 Individual languages and their relative powers

Essien (2003^b) has given the interplay of these powers arising from the dichotomy between majority and minority languages. What is a major or majority language and what is a minor or minority language? Can a minority language lord it over the majority ones? Or is it always the case that the majority language lords it over the minority ones?

Minority and Majority languages have been viewed from the perspective of demography or number of speakers and the domination or power of language in a given community. From a global view point Skutnabb-Kangas (1990) sees linguistic minority and majority in terms of power relationship, not in terms of numerical strength (though the two sometimes coincide). For her:

> If a 'majority' is used to refer to a numerically strong but politically weak group (like "the blacks" in South Africa, this is marked by calling them a 'powerless' majority, implying that they have the capacity and resources to become a 'real' majority (i.e. get access to their fair share of power and

resources). Several minorities, which together form a numerical majority and have approximately equal status when compared with each other, can also be seen as a majority. Groups like the white group in South Africa, which is numerically a minority, but in terms of power and majority can be marked by calling it a powerful minority'.

By this definition of language power, English spoken (though in our Nigerian way) by small ethnic elites in the country is markedly a powerful minority language, given its status as a dominant language, as defined later.

Put more simply, a language spoken by a relatively small number of people may become powerful and dominant because of the people who speak it. Powerful native speakers of a language-powerful in every sense of the word – invest their language with power and prestige. On the other hand, poor and unaccomplished people, no matter how numerous they may be, do very little to uplift their language.

However, Skutnabb-Kangas's definition of majority-minority languages is only part of the equation. Garry and Rubino (2001) see a majority language primarily in terms of numerical strength. For them, then, a language spoken by 2 million people or more is a world major language, regardless of the achievements of the speakers.

Using this criterion, then, there are only six major languages in Nigeria by world standard: Hausa, Yoruba, Igbo, Ibibio, Kanuri and Fulfulde, the language of the Fulani people. The rest are referred to as minority languages, again by world standard, though they vary in population, development and power or dominance.

But the concepts of majority and minority are often shifting-determined by each linguistic community speakers find themselves (e.g. a nation state in a federal set-up, etc). Therefore a language may be a minority in one setting, but a majority in another. For example Lokəə (spoken in Yakurr LGA) is a minority language in Cross River State but a major language in Yakurr LGA and while Hausa is a minority language in Ghana, in Nigeria it is clearly a major language (cf. Bamgbose 1992).

At this point, we introduce the notion of dominant language. This concept has been used loosely formally undefined by linguists even in sociolinguistics, and yet in any linguistic setting or situation, globally, it is the source of power. Fortunately Essien (2003[b]) has defined it in this way:

> In a bilingual or multilingual setting, there is usually one language, regardless of its size, which invests its users not only with what Wardhaugh (1986:344) refers to as "the full panoply of uses that signify a standard language" but also with prestige, self-confidence and power.

And by power here we mean economic, educational, academic, intellectual, socio-cultural and political powers.

In Nigeria, the language that does this, unfortunately, thanks to our abysmal ignorance of the nature of language and its powers, is English, often referred to as the exoglossic language.

The rest of the other languages have power of dominance in varying degrees-Hausa in the North. When you combine this with Arabic, the religious influence is simply stupendous. That is why all you need to inflame a community is the Hausa/Arabic translation of 'infidel'.

Yoruba used to dominate the old west directly but nowadays subtly, as typical of Oduduwa people. The influence of Igbo is obvious. However, as observed by Essien (2000b) the Igbo people were unable to impose their language on their fiercely independent minority populations. The minority persons who speak Igbo must have lived in Igbo land. A study by this inaugural lecture (cf. Essien 1979) revealed that Cross River State (then comprising what is now Akwa Ibom and Cross River) children who lived in minority areas, like Jos, in the North and Benin City, Bendel State (then) spoke Hausa and Yoruba, respectively. On the other hand, children from the North, West and even Igboland resident in Calabar and Uyo, the so-called minority area cities in Eastern Nigeria learnt and spoke Efik and Ibibio, respectively. I think one has to admit here that the Igbo are the most benevolent of the three major ethnic groups in respect to the treatment of their linguistic minorities.

If Hausa, Igbo and Yoruba are three major languages in Nigeria with varying degrees of power of dominance, there are other categories of languages variously classified as main, minority/Minor and small group by Bamgbose (1992); millionaire, centimil and minority/ local by Brann (1986); second class, third class and fourth class by Olagoke (1982) and medium, minor and micro-minor by Essien (forthcoming).

These classifications correspond not only to the sizes of the languages but also to respective dominance and power. Indeed Bamgbose (1992) was aware of this when he said this:

> With the creation of and recreation of states, languages, which were formerly called minority languages, have attained a dominant status. This is true of Urhobo in Delta, Igala in Kogi, Nupe in Niger and Ibibio in Akwa Ibom.

All these along with languages like Tiv, Efik, Edo, Ijaw, Kanuri, Fulfulde, etc., belong to Essien's medium category of languages.

But there are hundreds of minor and micro-minor languages, which are distressingly powerless, unstatusful and dominated, sometimes mercilessly. Most of them are spoken in the South-South and Middle-Belt areas. They include Agwagune, Echie, Koro, Eggon, to mention but a few. Some Nigerian linguists are so uncharitable as to recommend that such languages should be allowed to die a benign death (cf. Jibril 1990). That is how powerless some languages in this country are! For when your language dies, your people also die as a people with a distinct culture and heritage. And this is why UNESCO undertook the *World Languages Report* published in 2001. I am proud to say, Mr. Chairman that I have received a commendation from UNESCO in Spain for my collaboration described as "this essential collaboration."

2.7 Empowerment of powerless/weak Nigerian languages
Which are the weak or powerless Nigerian languages?

a. Numerically they have, by rule of thumb, less than 300,000 speakers.

b. Their domain of use is the home or close family circle. Even their usages are characterized by a growing phenomenon in Nigerian languages called code-mixing (e.g. Mmaaha Politics), further dispowering the languages.

c. They have no official or standard orthographies, or no orthography at all. Essien (1990) estimated that about 75% of Nigerian languages have no orthographies. That is, such languages are unwritten. People whose languages are unwritten are at a very low level of civilization. For as Essien (1985:3) has said, "Without a written language, a people cannot preserve their history, their ethos, their philosophies, their heroic deeds, their myths and their legends."

d. They lack basic pedagogical grammars and other developments such as primers and dictionaries, not to mention literacy traditions.

2.7.1 How to empower such languages

In Section six of this lecture, we saw that as each new nation in Europe became independent, the governments of such new nations wasted no time in developing the languages of their new nation states through language planning so that such languages might be able to serve these new nations more effectively in all aspects of communication. Even the older nations of Europe like England, France, Italy, Germany, etc. had to do that. It is Instructive, isn't it, to know that the most powerful languages in the world, the English language, French, Italian, etc. were described in these unflattering terms: "The vulgar tongues, immature, unpolished and limited in resources," about six centuries ago. These languages are what they are now, not because they were born so- incidentally no language was ever born a science language- it is made so by sheer efforts of human development. So these languages went through development by owners of the language and have become what they are. Today we say English is indispensable to us. May be. But who made it so?

So there is a great deal for us to learn from the histories of language development which can lead to the empowerment of not only the weakest of Nigerian languages but even for further development and empowerment of the so-called developed ones like Hausa, Igbo and Yoruba, not to mention others like Ibibio, Efik, Edo, Ijaw, etc.

Fortunately Essien (1990, 1998, 2000 and 2002) has been giving serious thoughts to the fate of these languages in matters of development and empowerment.

In 1986, in an explosive lead paper later published as Essien (1990) he outlined the basic steps of development and empowerment as follows:

(a) The provision of a standard orthography acceptable to the generality of the native speakers of the language.

(b) The production of primers for the primary school system.

(c) The compilation and publication of a dictionary.

(d) The production of general literacy materials and the creation of a literacy tradition.

(e) Translation of classics such as the Holy Bible into the language.

Other Essien (1990) recommendations include the role to be played by the government, especially in approving the orthographies for these languages officially and helping to fund the publication of primer series without which literacy would be impeded. Commercial publishers tend to shun publishing in the weak languages for obvious reasons.

A very important factor in empowerment is the attitude of the speakers of the language themselves. If you use your language and encourage your children to do so too, your language will survive. If people of the community, especially the outstanding and rich ones, funds language development projects, the government - local, state and even federal – will not ignore your laudable efforts.

I recommend the example of the Ibibio people in the 1980s. They devised and published the orthography of their language – the first people in Nigeria to do so. The state and federal Governments had no choice than to rush to assist them.

These steps and actions complemented by a positive attitude of the people will go a long way to empowering weak Nigerian languages and thereby enhancing their status locally and even nationally.

But perhaps the most enduring way to empower Nigerian languages – be they micro-minor, minor, medium or major-is to recognize a credit in a Nigerian Language at SSSCE (or its equivalent) as an alternative to English for general entry requirement into the university and other tertiary institutions in the country. In other words, it should be either a credit in English or a Nigerian language as a general requirement. In this way, by a stroke of the pen Nigerian languages would be enormously empowered.

For the first time, Nigerians would see the relevance for studying their mother tongues or even another Nigerian language. For as Essien (1981) has said:

> Until Africans can see the economic, educational political and social benefits for studying their languages, the study of these languages will remain largely, if not wholly academic.

2.8 Summary and conclusion

In this lecture, Mr. Chairman, we have been able to do the following, among other things:

a. We have demonstrated the divine origin and biological basis of language as well as defined it, the discipline that studies it and the concept of power, which language underlies.
b. We have discussed the various aspects of the powers of language- in communication, in persuasion, propaganda, diplomacy, and religion.
c. We have also highlighted the special problem of dispowered minor and micro-minor languages in Nigeria and suggested how to empower them. It is also suggested, for the first time, that a credit in a Nigerian language at the SSSCE (or its equivalent) be accepted as an alternative to English.

In conclusion, Mr. Chairman, Ladies and Gentlemen, because language is an attribute of God-He who made us fearfully and wonderfully also made us linguistically, endowing us genetically with a faculty of language, which enables us to possess language, regardless of race, nation, sex, creed, class or colour - we are innately powerful verbally. Therefore, nothing, nothing whatsoever should be done by any person, group, or authority wittingly, or unwittingly to weaken or dispower anybody's or community's language, the vital highway between God and man.

Chapter 3
Nigerian Languages and Empowerment

3.01 Preamble
By way of protocol, I would like to thank the Local Organising Committee of the 11th Annual Conference of Association of Nigerian Language Teachers (ANLAT), the Department of Linguistics, and the Executive Council of the Association for considering me qualified to present the keynote paper on this august occasion. For me it is a kind of home coming, for all my keynote and lead papers, until now, have been delivered elsewhere. I thank the Department of Linguistics for making this 'homecoming' possible, especially coming on the heels of the first ever festschrift organised in this University for a Professor. I apologise for amending the original title somewhat so as to make it more embracing.

3.1 Introduction
In this chapter, I will define Nigerian Languages and empowerment, consider the status quo of these languages and suggest ways to empower them.

3.2 Definitions
3.2.1 Nigerian languages
Nigerian Languages are those indigenous or native languages spoken within the geo-political boundaries of

the nation-state known as Nigeria derived etymologically from the River Niger, one of the great rivers of the country. Each of these languages, no matter the number of its speakers, has its own distinct cultural heritage and reveals a mental virtuosity which uniquely expresses the humanity of its speakers as God's creatures "fearfully and wonderfully made".

The number of these languages in the Nigerian polity, in my opinion, depends on one's definitions of **language** and **dialect** or some may say **lect**, definitions more often than not coloured by politics, ideology, bias and opportunism. Before the 1970s and the politics of separatism aided by Western historical or comparative linguists who, wittingly or unwittingly, appear to have emphasized differences among these languages, there were far fewer Nigerian languages than there are now. You need to read the works of late Kay Williamson, Bruce Connell, Roger Blench, etc. closely and critically to judge for yourself. The various estimates of the number of languages of Nigeria, nearly all of them given by foreigners, or based on their analyses, must therefore be consumed with care. Writing on the origins, birth and development of transformational generative grammar, Newmeyer (1980:xii) makes this frank admission.

Since there is no such utopia as totally unbiased historiography, it would be utopian to imagine that an author could be free from background assumptions or beliefs that colour his or her perception of events.

Vital Aspects of African Linguistics

When all the varieties in dialect clusters such as Ibibio-Efik, the Ejagham cluster, the Agwagwune cluster, etc are simply treated as separate and distinct languages, in spite of high percentage of cognacy and mutual intelligibility among speakers in each cluster, then there is more to it than just scholarship. In my opinion, the actual number of distinct languages spoken in this country is yet to be determined.

3.2.1.2 Commonness in Nigerian languages

Genetically, most Nigerian languages belong to the Niger-Congo family, branching into Benue-Congo (new), Ijoid, Mande, Gur, West Atlantic and Adamawa-Ubangian. Historical linguists, like Williamson (1989) under some new classification, say that most, if not all, the Nigerian languages formerly classified as Kwa have been merged with an enlarged Benue-Congo and referred to as 'new' Benue-Congo. Some comparativists (cf. Eze and Manfredi 2001) have, however, rejected this.

All Southern languages and a large chunk of Northern languages, including Fulfulde, are Niger Congo languages. Other families of languages represented in Nigeria are Afro-Asiatic, to which Hausa, a Chadic language and one of the three main languages, belongs; and Nilo-saharan, to which Kanuri, a Saharan language, belongs.

Phonologically, except Fulfulde (sometimes referred to as Fula), all known and described languages in Nigeria are tonal. That is such languages use pitch, like consonants and vowels, to contrast meanings of words.

Consonantally, many Nigerian Languages have syllabic nasals, i.e. nasal sounds constitute a syllabic peak or nucleus itself as a vowel does. Many Nigerian languages also have doubly articulated sounds like kp/gb while a few, like Hausa, have implosives like /ɗ/'.

Vocalically, vowels in Nigerian languages often exhibit the harmonic principle, a situation in which vowels in a two or more syllable word are so constrained as to occur in a compatible set. For example, in Igbo /i/ and /e/ can be selected in words on the basis of the ± ATR feature specification. Similarly, in Ibibio and Efik, what are phonetically known as front vowels get together while back vowels also do so in verbs of more than one syllable, as in dippe: 'lift up' and kunno: 'raise one's height in order to see better' in Ibibio. In these examples /i/ and /e/ in **dippe** and /u/ and /o/ in **kunno** are pairs of front and back vowels, respectively.

Not all Nigerian languages exhibit vowel harmony. For example, Hausa and Edo do not.

In addition to vowel harmony, vowel elision is also common in the phonologies of Nigerian languages. By vowel elision we mean a process by which some vowels are deleted or elided in certain environments, such as the following in Ibibio and Igbo:

(1a.) ké ụ́fộk = kúfộk 'at home'
(1b.) ná ụ́lọ̀ = n'ụ́lọ̀ 'at home'

At the level of word classes, nearly all Nigerian languages have ideophones, a

> ... class of words, often anomalous phonologically, ... whose semantic function is the intensification of a situation, or an apt picturesque, epigrammatic or sense-intensifying description (Essien 1990a).

Examples of ideophones in Ibibio are kpək and **ñwáñ** in the following sentences.

(2a) Éyò ákịm kpək:
'Night came all of a sudden'

(2b) Ánnám ñwáñ ké ídém:
'I felt a sudden sensation in my body'

At the level of syntax or sentence structure, serial construction is a common feature of Nigerian languages. A serial construction is a nuclear sentence with a double (or even triple) verb. Consider the following exmples in Ibibio.

3a) Ìmé ánam útóm ọ́nọ́ fédédád kófúmèn
'Ime works for the Federal Governemnt'

3b)   Dáá kpérè étó ókò
      'Stand near tree yonder' = 'Stand near yonder tree'

Where **ánám útóm ọ́nọ́** and **dáá kpérè** are the serial verbs. I am sure there are comparable constructions in other Nigerian languages.

3.3 Nigerian languages and classification according to size
If the actual number of distinct languages spoken in Nigeria has eluded linguists, classification of these languages according to sizes, i.e. number of speakers per each language, has not, even if the actual numbers are often inflated or reduced according to who controls the centre, for political reasons., The Nigerian census is a highly sensitive and political matter.

Be that as it may, three languages have since our political independence been always recognized as being major languages by reason of their respective numerical strength. These are Hausa, Igbo and Yoruba. The rest of the four or more hundred languages are then regarded as non-major or minority languages, regardless of their incomparably differing sizes. This is, unfortunately, what is entrenched in the nation's National Policy on Education (NPE), which controls our language planning and development policy and of which Essien is a well-known critic (cf. Essien 1990b, 2003a).

Departing from the NPE dichotomy of major-minority languages in Nigeria, Emenanjo (1986) divides Nigerian languages into three categories, namely **developed, developing** and **undeveloped,** according to language development criteria. Brann's (1986) division into decamillionaire (i.e. 10 million speakers and above), millionaire (i.e. between 1 and 9 million speakers), centimil (i.e. spoken by 100,000 or more people), and minority or local languages (i.e. spoken by less than 100,000 people) is based primarily on the numerical strength of each language. Olagoke's (1982) four categories of **first class, second class, third class and fourth class** are unfortunate labels but correspond more or less to Brann's classification. Bamgbose (1992) divides Nigerian languages into three namely **major, main** and **small group,** while Essien (2003c) does so into four: **major, medium, minor** and **micro-minor** more or less corresponding to Brann's classification based on numerical strength. Williamson's (1990) classification with which I have much to disagree, is concerned primarily with written texts such as the orthography, the Bible, etc and the media use of the languages but excluding grammars written in English. Yet she was largely ignorant of what was happening in some of these languages and came up with a distorted picture of their development status.

What do these classifications signify?

a. They remind us that the issue raised by Essien in 1986 in Maiduguri published in 1990 cannot be wished away- they are still with us. This is why

Essien (2003a) suggests that the number of major languages based on world definition of a major language be raised, since only major languages seem to enjoy federal government attention. At the same time all non-major but viable languages would be a joint responsibility of the federal, state and local governments to develop. Let no-one be left in doubt- the development of any language no matter how small it may be is in the overall interest of the growth and development of the entire nation, for the chain is an strong as its weakest link.

b. The classification by Williamson (1990) in particular reveals the paucity of written material in all the minority languages, something which should be of serious concern to all tiers of government, since language is a mirror of the mind (cf. Radford 1988). A language which is not properly developed is a poor image of the mind. So a situation in which a person lives in the 21st century but his language has little or no contact with developments in that century is very tragic indeed, especially for an oil-rich nation like ours.

c. Even the three major languages are not immune to the fate of the minority languages, because the only way for a language, major, medium, minor, or micro-minor to survive anywhere in the world is to be used in all forms of communication that a modern society requires. Excluding Nigerian languages from the mainstream of life ... education at all levels, government at the executive, legislative, and judiciary levels ... trade, commerce, industry, information technology, socio-cultural affairs and life in general as we live in our various communities is the surest way to kill these languages- all of them!

3.4 Empowerment

We define power, from which empowerment is derived, non-technically as simply strength, might, ability to compel some individual, authority, control, a right, dominance or domination (cf. Essien 2003b). Power, which usually flows from authority, can be divine, political, legal, military, educational, cultural, physical, sexual, religious, etc. to mention the most obvious. When an entity (or a group of entities) human or non-human, which previously had no power, is strengthened, fortified, energized - indeed given power or status- it is empowered. Sometimes power is taken by force as in a coup d'etat by the military.

How many Nigerian languages are being used as a subject as well as a medium of instruction at even the primary school level? This is what the Ife Pilot Project (cf. Fafunwa 1989) provided the empirical evidence for. In village primary schools perhaps the major languages and some of the medium languages are being used. But in cities, I doubt even if the major languages are taught at all. The fact of the matter is that our NPE recommends the use of the mother tongue as a medium of instruction only in the first three years of primary education. Besides, the overwhelming domination and influence of English does not allow Nigerian languages a breathing space. So our languages remain powerless even at the primary school level. If the languages are not used systematically, except perhaps the three major ones, how can the appropriate meta-language be developed for these languages beginning at this level? The Japanese empower their language right from the primary school but we teach our primary school children, not in their mother tongue, but in a second language. And this is the result of empowerment and lack of it, as reported by Olarenwaju (nd)

> Evidence from the Second International Science Study showed that Japanese primary school came first in primary science among the countries of the world with Nigerian pupils among last (STAN 1992).

This report speaks for itself

At the Secondary school level, some medium languages like Ibibio and Efik can be offered to the JSS level while the three major languages can be up to the SSS, NCE and degree levels. But these are not important options, as observed by Essien (1993).

In Colleges and Universities, students of Nigerian languages hardly respect these languages nor do such students appear to have confidence in themselves that what they study is worthwhile. They are often looked down upon as poor students who could not make it elsewhere. In what is now the University of Uyo, for example, students who read Ibibio or Efik for a degree are often ridiculed as "mbio una se enam", ie 'those who lack what to study'.

Nor do parents help matters at all. In most so-called educated homes, at least in Akwa Ibom and Cross River States, English is now the medium of expression, the English of the servant or maid notwithstanding.

In churches and other religious gatherings, even in remote villages, Nigerian languages hold a secondary position: the message must be delivered in English and then translated as best as it can be into the language of the community.

In the electronic media, the use of Nigerian languages is severely restricted: limited to news translation and some magazine programmes. In Akwa Ibom State, for example, the State radio and television stations do not even permit news translation to complement their other laudable indigenous language programmes. At the national level, the use of Nigerian languages is an apology. And this is because the dominant language, English, has taken over the most important programmes that interest the elite. In entertainment, especially the movies, English takes a commanding position. Yet the Indian movie industry has shown that a third world country can have a thriving movie industry in its own language. I can go on and on but I think enough has been given to show that Nigerian languages are in need of empowerment, perhaps in varying degrees.

3.5 What happened to language development projects?

In answering this question, we will have empowerment as our focus.

In 1978, a national workshop on scientific and mathematical terminologies in nine Nigerian languages- Hausa, Igbo, Yoruba, Edo, Efik, Fulfulde, Izon, Kanuri and Tiv – was held at the University of Ife, now Obafemi Awolowo University with the objective of producing a glossary of these terms for primary schools in the nation. After nine years, *A Vocabulary of Primary Science and Mathematics in Nine Nigerian Languages* was produced in three volumes by the National Language Centre of the Federal Ministry of Education, Science and Technology in 1987. According to the then Minister in his forward, "The Centre is responsible for systematic development and promotion of Nigerian Languages in education and the three volumes were a response to this need." Closely following these volumes was a quadrilingual dictionary of legislative terminologies in Hausa, Igbo and Yoruba. These developments held out great hope for the enrichment or elaboration of our languages for their empowerment. What has gone wrong?

The Centre has since been succeeded by the Language Development Centre of the Nigeria Educational and Research Development Council (NERDC) and running parallel with it is the National Institute for Nigerian Languages, Aba. On Language Development Centre, Nwachukwu (2003) has raised an issue which has been agitating my mind. He says:

> During the tenure of Professor Babatunde Fafunwa as Federal Minister, language education in particular and educational research in general received a lot of support from the federal government. During this period, two units of the Federal Ministry of Education-the National Language Centre and the Educational Research Unit were merged into what is now known as the Nigeria Educational and Research Development Council (NERDC) as a Ministry of Education parastatal. It is not yet clear whether the merger has benefited the language unit, but what is clear is each of the executive directors of the Council has been a professor of Education and the language unit has been very quiet of late, it seems to be in a state of suspended animation.

With the language Development Centre in Abuja said to be "in a state of suspended animation", how can Nigerian languages be effectively put on the path of empowerment?

Of the National Institute for Nigerian Languages (NINLAN), Aba, Nwachukwu (ibid:24) makes another observation with which I agree:

> The establishment of the National Institute for Nigerian Languages (NINLAN) has been greeted as a great milestone in our efforts to accord our indigenous languages their rightful position in the scheme of things. But most of the scholars with whom I have discussed the subject have been surprised by the way the establishment has been run for nearly ten years of its existence. To put it mildly, the affairs of NINLAN appear to have been shrouded in secrecy; certainly nearly all the knowledgeable scholars who ought to contribute ideas on how best to run the Institute so that it fulfils the goals and objectives of those who set it up have been excluded from its affairs.

No wonder, then, Nigerian languages, especially the so-called minority ones, remain where they are developmentally- little more than tribal languages in an age of computer and information technology. Yet clearly as the minister said the objective of the terminology project, which started in the 1970s, "is that Nigerian languages will constantly be enriched and made adaptable to the socio-economic realities of our national development. It is also the desire of the Ministry that every child should be socialized through his mother tongue or the language of the immediate community". (Federal Ministry of Education 1987). It is unfortunate that there has been no follow up of what the National Language Centre seriously planned for: the systematic development, promotion and empowerment of Nigerian Languages in education.

3.6.0 Language as a mirror of the mind and culture
3.6.1 Language as a mirror of the mind

Linguist familiar with Chomsky's theory of grammar know that the basis of language acquisition by a child is a genetically endowed language faculty in the mind or brain which incorporates "a set of principles of Universal Grammar – in the sense that the language faculty must be such as to allow the child to develop grammar of a natural language on the basis of suitable linguistic experience of the language" (Radford 1997:10). Exposure to a particular language "serves as an input to principles of UG which are an inherent part of the child's language faculty [in the mind], and UG then provides the child with an algorithm [i.e. a descriptive apparatus] for developing a grammar [of the language]." We can therefore say that one's competence or knowledge or grammar of one's language is a mirror of the mind.

If language is a mirror of the mind, then all Nigerian languages are mirrors of the minds of the speakers of their respective languages. That means the structural or grammatical principles and rules universally present in them as human languages and parametrically (i.e. with respect to their individual characteristics including even genetic, areal, typological ones), are also mirrored. This is something too weighty, too serious, too awesome, too fundamental and too close to the soul, psyche and our sacredness as human species to be toyed with. The defining characteristic of language compels us to embrace our multilingualism for all the Nigerian languages contain our collective wisdom, experiences and man's eternal quest to cope with his environment and please his creator.

3.6.2 Language as a mirror of culture

Language is both a cultural index and the expression of that index. When you are learning a language you are entering the cultural domain and terrain of the native speakers of the language. You get to understand the belief system, the taboos, the totems, the values, the ethos, the fears and hopes, the foods, the traditions, the clothes, the ceremonies, the names and the naming system and whatever identifies the people by way of their mental and creative outputs: religion, literature and the arts in general, economic well-being, education etc. This is indeed an enormous power of language.

But how do Nigerian Languages make use of this power? Is it by surrendering it to the all powerful, dominating and intimidating English as they are doing currently? I shouldn't think so. For us to continue to do so is tantamount to the genocide of our God-given gifts together with their invaluable heritages. It would be very tragic because most of those languages (cf. Essien 1990b) are either unwritten or have very lean written literature. So what do we do?

3.7 Suggestions

The most practical suggestion I am making for the eternal benefit of all Nigerian languages is that all segments of the Nigerian nation should begin to systematically and seriously use them in areas or fields from which they have been previously systematically excluded, for use is the only way of causing languages to serve the community in which it is rooted efficiently. (Essien 1979)

First, let us set a target date in which we will begin to use our viable mother tongues to teach at the primary school level. The Six-year Primary Project (SYPP) of the Institute of Education, University of Ife, now Obefemi, Awolowo University blazed the trail and gave us the empirical basis that all primary school subjects can be taught and understood successfully in a Nigerian language. Similarly, the Primary Education Improvement Projects

(PELP) of the Institute of Education, Ahmadu Bello University, Zaria independently confirmed it. The 1978 national workshop in Ife practicalized the enrichment of Nigerian languages programme. Indeed as a pilot scheme it was quite successful. This is why the then minister of Education himself said this: "The long-term goal of this sort of project is that Nigerian languages will constantly be enriched and made adaptable to the socio-economic realities of our National development" (cf. Federal Ministry of Education 1987).

My own target date is today, here and now. From now on, let every university- federal, state, and private - start a language elaboration or enrichment programme in at least a Nigerian language leading to the development of a meta-language for each language. Given the number of universities in this country, quite a sizeable number of languages will begin to receive empowerment. To ensure some form of co-ordination of these projects, this Association, LAN and Association of Promotion of Nigerian Languages can pull their resources together and hold workshops from time to time so that individual groups can compare notes, encourage and strengthen each other and thereby benefit from each other.

What these departments (and/or Institutes) would be doing would augment what the two federal establishment should have been doing all along. The French language was developed by the French academy established as long ago as 1635. Our own language establishments should follow the example of the French academy, which was a deliberate and systematic French government involvement. If our two federal government bodies have not done this, it is high time they did so. In fact, language groups or associations in the country should be resorting to them in matters of language development, if they, particularly the non-major ones, heed the advice of Essien (1990b:167-168).

It is, however, one thing to enrich and elaborate each Nigerian language as suggested above and quite another for these languages to be used in situations or areas from which they have been hitherto excluded. This has arisen from the overwhelming influence of the English language. No-one is suggesting the proscription of English. Far from it, but we are facing a very critical situation in our national existence in which our own languages, as have been observed by many well-meaning and knowledgeable people, are facing the awesome prospect of becoming imperceptibly extinct. The way I see the development of our linguistic situation, we may very well be another Australia in the making, minus the Union Jack. For how else can you envisage the future when most educated young parents speak only English to their children at home, pay exorbitant fees for them at **English only** speaking schools and prevent these children from 'contamination' with their native language, the very languages with which these parents grew up and socialized. There is bound to be a crisis of identity, if there hasn't been one already, for no Nigerian child can grow up to become a true Nigerian with an English or American mind set. What I cannot understand is what has overwhelmed the collective mind of Nigerians so much that they lose sight of the fact that their children can be truly bilingual-speaking both the English language and their own respective mother tongues fluently simply by having them exposed equipollently to the two languages.

Perhaps at this point we should revisit our attitudes to our languages. There is nothing wrong intrinsically in learning another language in this case a language as rich as English but there is a whole lot that is wrong when the second language, rather augmenting, is supplanting our language repertoire. Essien (1993) has given useful hints on what should be done to enhance the status of our languages and thereby empower them. Some of these are worth repeating for emphasis.

a. All Policy provisions in relation to Nigerian languages in the NPE should be fully implemented. As it is commonly known and has actually been pointed out by a number of well-known Nigerian linguists, like Bamgbose (1982) and Essien (1990b), there is quite often a dichotomy between what is provided for in theory in a policy statement and what is in fact done.

b. The government should make it mandatory for Nigerian languages to be used actively in those vital areas of our national development from which they had long been excluded. These include areas such as higher education, science and technology, information technology, one of the so-called new humanities, research, computer, commerce and industry, the three arms of government, the arts and culture-indeed the entire gamut of the Nigerian society. A language is as important, virile and living as the community or society in which it is spoken. One of the most costly mistakes the governments and people of Nigeria have made in the more than forty decades for our nationhood has been the exclusion, wittingly or unwittingly, of Nigerian languages from the vital areas of development, as Essien in a number of publications has drawn the nation's attention to (cf. Essien 1977, 1979, 1993, 2003a, 2005, etc.).

c. Now that nursery education is becoming increasingly popular in the country and nursery schools are found even in villages, there should be a government policy making it mandatory for all properly registered nursery schools throughout the country to teach at least a Nigerian language alongside English. This is essential because nursery schools are attended by children from elitist homes whose parents, in many cases, use English only at home in an obvious attempt to prevent such children from contact with Nigerian languages, which are erroneously viewed as inferior and unhelpful. This will go a long way to show the value of the languages and create a corresponding sense of value in the children. In the long run it is hoped that this will help to produce better adjusted educated young Nigerians with pride in themselves and their mother tongues.

d. Today in many government offices and schools, the major language of the state is used informally, which is quiet an interesting development. For example in Akwa Ibom State, Ibibio is commonly spoken in ministries, parastatals and schools. In Calabar, the State Capital of Cross River State, Efik is used in much the same way. I am almost certain that this is the case in all Igbo, Yoruba and Hausa and Kanuri states. I would like to suggest that the uses of these languages be formalized in these states, respectively. In this way, more and more areas from which these Nigerian languages have been previously excluded will have them back.

e. Nigerian authors who write in English should reconsider their stance in writing their literary works. Wole Soyinka and Chinua Achebe, our great literary giants, owe us something. Chaucer wrote in English in Medieval England, at a time when the English language was very socially inferior to Norman French. Today he is the father of English literature. Why would our literary laureates not imitate this beautiful example of indigenous and low language promotion? Consider what Wardhaugh has said in this connection.

For about three centuries after the Norman Conquest in 1066, English and Norman French co-existed in England in a diaglossic situation the H variety and English the L. However, gradually the L variety assumed more and more functions associated with the H so that by Chaucer's time it became conceivable that a major literary work could be cast in L.

It is high time Soyinka and Achebe wrote their next works in Yoruba and Igbo, respectively.

f. In 1993, I advocated the following. The teachers of Nigerian languages should come together to form an association to fight for certain benefits and the promotion of the languages. Such an association should be registered as a professional body like those of Mathematics, Science and English teachers.

I am exceedingly gratified to see the Association of Nigerian Languages Teachers (ANLAT) with all that is has achieved so far including this 11th Annual Conference. I believe that with NINLAN, where ANLAT is appropriately based, the Language Development Centre, Association for the Promotion of Nigerian Languages, LAN and all lovers of their mother tongues, Nigerian languages will take their rightful places in our national, state and local government affairs.

Finally, I would like to end this paper with the suggestion I made in my inaugural lecture (cf. 2003b:37).

Perhaps the most enduring way to empower Nigerian languages - be they micro-minor, minor, medium or major- is to recognize a credit in a Nigerian Language at SSCE (or its equivalent) as an alternative to English for general entry requirement into the university and other tertiary institutions in the country. In this way by a stroke of the pen Nigerian languages would be enormously empowered. For the first time, Nigerians would see the practical relevance for studying their mother tongue or even another Nigerian language.

For as Essien (1981) modified has said: "Until Africans can see the economic, educational, political and social benefits for studying their languages, there would be little point studying such inconsequential and powerless languages, as most of our languages are currently viewed.

Chapter 4
Syntax-Phonology Interface in African Languages

4.0 Introduction

Commonly, phonology and syntax are viewed as two seemingly distant or little related areas having little interlacing or interlinking system of relationship. We are so familiar with the intimacy between phonetics and phonology that we are very comfortable with the latter being described as "functional phonetics" by Abercrombie (1967). At the same time, there is no problem with the relationship between phonology and morphology, hence the term morphophonemics. Not to mention the straight forward relationship between morphology and syntax, hence morpho-syntax. Need I mention the marriage between syntax and semantics? That's why Chomsky quickly reversed himself after his *Syntactic Structures,* which excluded semantics from syntax.

Yet do we have to go too far to see the obvious relationship between syntax and phonology in the following six sentences below for those of us who speak English?

(1) a. He gave me a book
(1) b. I gave him a book
(2) a. They told John the story
(2) b. John told them the story.

(3) a. She hid it from us
(3) b. We hid it from her

Do we therefore have phono-syntax, if you permit our audacity?

This paper attempts:

(i) To investigate the relationship between phonology and syntax in general in African languages.
(ii) To revisit the issue of syntactic conditioning of tense allomorphs independently arrived at by Essien and Zima in a number of their publications.
(iii) To use this opportunity to reappraise some analysis of focus in African languages.

4.2.0 Phonology and syntax
4.2.1 Phonology

Phonology is the sound system or pattern of a human or natural language. Unlike phonetics, which is concerned with the study of speech sounds- their production by the articulatory organs, their physical characteristics as waves through the air (or some fluid), and their auditory perception by hearer/listener – in general or of a particular language, phonology is concerned primarily with the sound pattern or organization of individual languages, though not without some cross language considerations.

Phonology can be viewed from a number of theoretical stand points such as generative phonology, autosegmental phonology, phonemic theory, lexical phonology, etc.

In recent years, generative grammarians have linked phonology to Universal Grammar (UG), man's innate endowment. According to Kenstowicz (1994:2),

> Phonology is the component of linguistic knowledge that is concerned with the physical realization of language. Possession of this knowledge permits us to realize words and the sentences they compose as speech... and to recover them from the acoustic signal.

But this physical realization is based on the input from the syntactic component. Thus, according to Radford (1997:31),

> It would not be possible to provide a systematic account of English inflectional morphology unless we were to posit that words belong to grammatical categories and that a specific category of inflection attaches only to a specific category of word.

So clearly phonology and syntax are interwoven. From the early days of what is now described as classical generative phonology, pioneered by Noam Chomsky and Morris Halle (cf. Chomsky and Halle 1968), the phonology of a language has always been viewed as an integral part of grammar comprising the three major components of syntax, semantics and phonology. One of the strongest points raised against the phonemic theory was the insistence by its practitioners on the separation of phonology from grammar, then understood to mean morphology and syntax. The phonemicists referred to the non-separation as "mixing of levels" (cf. Hyman 1975:76-78). This is why Postal (1968) describes the approach as "autonomous phonemics."

To illustrate the integrativeness of the grammatical system of a language, generative grammarians see its (cf. Haegeman 1994) organization as follows:

4(i) Lexicon,
(ii) Syntax;
      (a) Categorial component;
      (b) Transformation component

(iii) PF – Component (Phonetic Form)
(iv) LF – Component (Logical Component)

Talking of integration of components and sub-components, the lexicon itself is a very fine example of it, specifying the abstract morphophnological structure of each lexical item and its syntactic features, including its categorical and contextual features. Is there still any doubt about the relationship between syntax and phonology in a grammatical system?

The rules of the categorical component meet some $\bar{X}$ theory criteria or conditions. Systems (4i) and (4iia) – i.e. the lexicon and the categorical component of syntax- already interlaced with semantic, phonological and syntactic features, constitute the base in a GB grammar. The base generates D-structures through lexical insertion into the structure generated by (4iia), in accordance with their features. These are mapped to s-structure by Move & leaving traces code-indexed by their antecedents. This rule constitutes the transformational component (4iib) and may appear in the PF and LF components. Thus the syntax generates S-structures which are assigned PF- and LF-representations by components. (4iii) and (4iv). So we can see how the rules – syntactic, semantic and phonological – are integrated, a fact that supports our analysis later on.

4.2.2 Syntax

Syntax is the study of grammar or language at the level of sentence (cf. Essien 1990:129ff). It is concerned with the combinatory principles of morphemes and words in the sentences of a language to make meaning. This is why Crystal (1995) defines syntax as "the way in which words are arranged to show relationships of meaning within (and sometimes between sentences). The term itself comes from the Greek word **Syntaxis**, meaning, "arrangement". So, even choreographers use syntax in their own way. In linguistics, "syntax examines the component parts or constituents of sentences of a language, the order in which they occur or must occur and their interdependencies that produce well-formed and meaningful sentences". (cf. Essien 1990a:129). One important aspect of the study of syntax is that we know that words belong to different categories and these categories have different distributions (cf. Radford 1997:32). Different syntactic distributions often result in different phonological realizations as we have seen in 1-3 above in different inflectional and derivational realizations at the phonological level.

Furthermore, there is now sufficient evidence that in many African languages syntax can and does intervene directly in the phonological shapes of some morphemes as we shall see later.

4.3 Phonology and syntax in African languages

Our concern with phonology and syntax in this conference compels us to look at these two broad areas in African languages more closely. And we are glad to say that the suprasegmentals or autosegmentals, depending on one's orientation, offer an interesting bridge between the two. In this regard, let us begin with our first objective, the relationship between syntax and phonology in general in African languages by considering tone, one of the commonest autosegmentals in African languages.

4.4 Tone

Tone has been defined as contrastive pitch, a phenomenon arising from the vibration of the vocal bands. For Welmers (1973:80), "a tone language is a language in which both pitch phonemes and segmental phonemes enter into the composition of at least some morphemes". In spite of this definition, there are still some unfortunate remarks made by some prejudiced linguists about tones. According to Welmers (1973:77), "a shocking number of people concerned with African languages still seem to think of tone as a species of esoteric, inscrutable languages – a sort of cancerous malignancy afflicting an otherwise normal linguistic organism". This can be said also of ideophones. Yet as we shall see presently, tones are acquired in much the same way as traditional sound segments, as a child is exposed to a linguistic experience, except that pitch as tone performs a different function from pitch as stress and intonation in English.

Let us now examine tone a little more closely. Clearly tone is primarily a phonological matter. But as a contrastive pitch it serves a lexical function in much the same way as a consonant or vowel does. And whether one views it as a suprasegmental or Goldsmith's (1976) autosegmental, the child learns it as part of a lexical item itself a result of arrangement.

But tone also performs a grammatical function in most tonal languages. For example in Ibibio, tone enters into composition, to use Welmers's expression, with some vowels or syllabic nasals to create personal concord morphemes, as in the following examples:

(6) a. Àmì ńdò ówó :   'I am a person'
(6) b. Àfò òdò ówó :   'You are a person'
(6) c. Ènyé ódò ówó: 'He/she/ is a person'
(7) a. Ńnyịn ìdò ówó: 'We are people
(7) b. Ńdùfò èdò ówó: 'You are people
(7) c. Òmmô èdò owo: 'They are people'

where /´/, /¯/, /`/ on the syllabic nasal [n], represents the first person singular, the next vowel prefix [o] in (6b) represents the second person singular, and the prefix vowel [o] in (6c), represents the 3rd person singular, respectively. Without the tonal differential, it would be impossible to distinguish between the second and the third person concord markers, even in dialects using {a-} vowel prefix, instead of {o-}. Similarly, in the plural examples, the difference between the second person and the third person would be impossible to show without a tonal differentiation. This is a very fine example of tonal use in which phonology (or tonology) and syntax directly relate to each other. At the lexical level, tone co-operates with consonantal and vocalic segments to create meaning. At the grammatical level tone participates in grammatical processes phono-syntactically. In Ibibio and many other Lower Cross Languages, this sometimes leads to the economy of words, in comparison with English. So instead of creating function words such as am, is, are etc, in English, a particular tonal melody embodies their functions, as the translation of the following sentences show:

(8)a. Mfèghè ìtók (1b):   'I am running'
(8)b. Mfèhè ìtók (EF):   'I am running'

As the examples above show, the particular tonal melody High-low on the concord marker and the first vowel of the root of the verb, mark the progressive or incompletive aspect, something many analysts of the two languages are often ignorant of. In many Ibibio dialects the preferred melody is High-Falling (i.e. mfêghè). So we can see in this way tonal melodies create their own syntax, i.e. their own arrangement.

4.4.1 Morphophonemic tone rules

Even more important as an indication of the interface between phonology and syntax are the tonal phenomena that Hyman (1975:224-5) refers to as morphophonemic tone rules. According to him (p. 224),

> In addition to phonetic rules of tonal assimilation and simplification, tone languages are characterized by numerous grammatical rules. These all have in common that they refer to specific morphemes and constructions.

For example, consider the role of tone in the syntax of associative construction in Igbo and Ibibio. In Igbo, according to Hyman (1975:223), there is an underlying floating high tone between two nouns below to produce the associative construction translated into English as "a monkey's jaw".

(9) a /agbá ˈ ènwè /: `a monkey's jaw'
(9) b = [agbá ènwè]

The floating high tone is assigned to the left to produce the construction in (9b) (at least in Central Igbo). In Ibibio, a similar construction is handled a little differently as the underlying and derived structures below show,

(10) a. /úkód ˈ ébód/: the leg of a goat'
(10) b. [úkód ébòd]: the leg of a goat'

In these examples, the underlying floating high tone causes tonal perturbation by which the floating high tone applies on the first syllable of **ébód** but changes nothing while the second tone is polarized or contrasted – perturbation indeed. Welmers (1973) has made a fairly simple tonal phenomenon in Efik unnecessarily complicated because apparently he didn't have enough data to indicate that Efik, like Ibibio, as pointed out in 4, marks the progressive aspect tonally.

In the Fante variety of Akan, the major language of Ghana, the difference between what is referred to as the habitual negative and optative forms of verbs are marked by tone, as stated by Dolphyne (1988:68) below:

> The negative prefix is a low tone nasal consonant, and the optative prefix is a High tone nasal. The difference between the Habitual Negative and the Optative forms of the verb is carried by tone:

Habitual Negative	Optative
Kòfí nkó	Kòfí ńkó
`Kofi does not go	'Let kofi go'

These examples and many more that time does not permit us to present show that through tone, phonology plays a very significant role making it virtually impossible for it to be divorced from grammar.

4.4 Interaction of phonology and syntax in tense morphology
4.5.1 Preliminary remarks

Essien observed the alternation of allomorphs of tense morphemes in Ibibio at an African Linguistic Conference in Montreal in Quebec, Canada in 1982 (cf. Essien 1983a). In that paper, he pointed out that the past tense, the present tense, and the future tense morphemes have allomorphs respectively which are conditioned by sentence types in the language, types categorized as Type 1 and Type II. In addition, each of these two types has categories which actually condition the selection of the alternants and these are yes/no-wh-question, positive/negative declarative sentences, neutral/emphatic constructions, and modally marked sentences. He identified the tense markers as follows.

II		Neutral	Non-neutral
(a)	Past	Màá-	Ké-
(b)	Present	Mé-	ɸ
(c)	Future	yàá/yáá-	dîî-

Then he presented this interesting distributional equivalence maá-: ké-what mé-: ɸ and what yàá/yáá-: dîî- But Hyman and Watters (1984), apparently unaware of Essien (1983a), introduced the notion of auxiliary focus and used it to account for similar phenomena found in Efik using, the features of [+ focus] and [- focus]. Unfortunately what is commonly regarded as [+ focus] markers, to use their own term, is used to specify what are in fact [- focus], as the following table taken from them shows.

	[- focus]	[+ focus]
PAST	- KV	- ma
PRESENT	ɸ	-mV – [-PROG]
FUTURE	di	- ye – [+ PROG]

And even more unfortunately, the Efik examples to illustrate [+ focus] and [- focus] auxiliaries are inaccurate and do not come from ordinary sentences in the language but from supposed answers to supposed questions. A full-scale discussion on the paper is beyond our scope but suffice it to say that the notion of auxiliary focus is noted and we may revisit it later.

While Oliveira (2004) correctly identifies the markers in Ibibio that are [+ focus], her analysis of the Ibibio tense system is markedly flawed. She anchors her arguments on the fact that the present tense marker, as clearly shown below,

(12) a Ḿ-mé – yàiyá:
   Ist per-pres-pretty =   `I'm pretty'

   b. Ḿ-màá - yàiyá
   1st per-past – pretty =   'I was pretty'

   c Ńyàá – yàiyá =   'I will be pretty'
   1st per-fut pretty

does not appear in type II sentences. She therefore concludes thus:- "Therefore I maintain that Ibibio does not grammaticalize "present tense", otherwise it should have a specific marker for Type II for the present form in the language."

One doesn't need to go too far to see that Oliveira missed the point. First the paradigm above – and many more examples of this type abound – shows that there is a [-foucs] present tense marker. The **mé**- in ḿméyàíyá cannot, by any stretch of imagination be construed as a perfect/perfective marker, as she has argued in her work. What she has actually missed is the fact that there are two morphemes in Ibibio which are homonymous, namely the present tense marker mé in static situations (Essien 1990b:67) and the immediate past tense marker often combined with perfect/perfective aspect meaning. Indeed Essien (1983b) has shown that homonymy is a common feature of Ibibio morphology. Consider the following examples to illustrate the point just made.

13) a Àmì ḿmédiòǫñó ènyé:
    I know him"

13) b. Àmì ḿmékóód ènyé
    I have called him"

In (13a) the speaker knows the individual at the moment of speaking. Period. This can be contrasted with (14a) below:

14) a. Ami mmàdiǫ̀ǫ̀ñǫ ènyé:
    `I knew him (but probably don't know him now)'

where the situation of knowing is prior to the moment of speaking. The speaker may not know the fellow now.

In (13b) the situation of speaking and calling are not simultaneous as are those of speaking and knowing in (13a). Second, we would like to draw the attention of the reader to the distribution equivalence in which me-: Φ what màá:- ke and what yáà-/yáà-: dîi-

Thirdly, in Linguistics, as in any science Φ has a value. For example:

Sheep + Φ = Plural sheep
Put + Φ = put + past

Readers are requested to consult Essien 1983a, 1990a and 1990b for full facts and arguments of Ibibio as a tripartite tense system as we return to our main point in 6 below.

4.6.0 Auxiliary focus or syntactic conditioning of tenses?

In English we are used to looking at tense with its morphological realizations in terms of allomorphs which are either phonologically or morphologically conditioned. In many African languages, however, there is what is referred to as a curious interplay between tense (or tense/aspect) and focus (cf. Hyman and Watters (1984:233) on the one hand, and what is regarded as syntactic intervention in phonology by Essien and Zima. Hyman and Watters go on to say this:

While the exact realization of this interplay varies from language to language, in each case some parameter of focus determines which of the two corresponding sets of these tense-aspect markers is used in a given situation.

In this way, the feature [+ focus] can be used to characterize some constructions depending on what is assumed to be focused.

On the other hand Essien and Zima in a series of publications (cf. Essien 1983a, 1990a, 1990b, 1991a, 1991b, 1995, etc and Zima 1967, 1971, 1985, 1986, 1995) individually and independently see some higher level of conditioning of allomorphs or alternants.

Let us begin with the summary of Essien's position. According to him, the Ibibio tense system is characterized as follows:

(a) It is a three-way opposition of past, present, and future.

(b) The past is represented by the allomorph or variant **màá-** or **ké-** the occurrence of which is determined by the absence or presence of categories such as negation, wh-question, mood, inceptive and progressive aspects, and some form of emphasis or focus.. In Hyman and Watters's analysis, these categories fall into [-focus] or [+ focus] used in specifying the auxiliary or what would in GB be regarded as IP (Inflectional Phrase).

(c) The future tense is represented by yàá-/yaá- or dîi- the occurrence of which is conditioned by the absence or presence of the same set of categories- negation, wh-question, mood, inceptive and progressive aspects, and some form of emphasis (or focus in Hyman and Watters's terminology).

(d) The present tense is represented by me – or zero allomorph (Φ). Interestingly, the same set of environments that determine the occurrence of màá- and yàá/yáà- also determine the occurrence of mé- and the environments that determine the occurrence of ké and dîi- also determine the occurrence of the zero allomorph of the present tense. In the present tense case, therefore, the alternation is between the presence and the absence of an overt market, something that eluded Oliveira (2004).

(e) There is a distribution equivalence of the allomorphs as stated before such that me-: Φ: what màá-: ké- and what yàá-/yáà-: dîi-

He further demonstrated that while mé-, màá- and yàá-/yáà, sometimes referred to as neutral allomorphs or variants, occur in what, he calls type 1 sentences, Φ, ké- and dîi- occur in complimentary distribution syntactically in what he refers to as Type II sentences, respectively. Type I sentences are sentences which contain a simple affirmation or a question which requires the answer yes or no (cf. Essien 1983a: 330). Type II sentences, on the other hand, contain categories like negation, mood, wh-question, etc, categories which in Hyman and Watters's analysis trigger focus on the auxiliary.

Zima, on his own, has given one of the clearest examples of the alternation of verbal forms conditioned, in our views, by the syntax of the Hausa language. According to him (Zima 1967:189),

> Some... sets of morphemes are in contrastive distribution with others, other sets are supposed to be in a particular kind of complimentary syntactic distribution. Some sets are, therefore, to be considered as full morphemes but other sets are supposed (or suspected) to be syntactic alternants.

Then he goes on to show (p. 190) the clearest instance of syntactic alternation in the tense/aspect system of Hausa, a Chadic language, saying:

> The most clear example case of syntactic alternation is obviously represented by **Sunáá** and **sukèè** forms. As discovered by many authors, those two forms are used in Hausa in complementary distribution. The Sukèè form occurs in a sum of environments which may be defined as follows:

(a) the so-called relative constructions, e.g. Mtààneⁿ dá sukèè shigaa daakì ``The people who are entering the room (= house).

(b) The so-called emphatic constructions Audu Sukèè neemaa `It is Audu they are seeking (not Haruna, e.g.)'

(c) Questions introduced by interrogative words particles, e.g.
Mèè sukèè neemaa
`What are they seeking?

Although Zima does not give actual examples in which the sunàà (i.e. the [- focus] form in Hyman and Watters's parlance) occurs, it is clear that this form will not occur in those sentences in which sukèè (i.e. the [+ focus] form occurs, namely relative, emphatic and wh-question construction environments identical to those in which the so-called contrastive (or [+ focus]) forms ké, Φ and dîi occur in Ibibio, as we have already pointed out in 4.5.1 above. In fact in Ibibio- and Efik too – a relative construction is one of the ways of emphasizing or focusing an item, as Essien (1983a) has pointed out.

The complementary distribution of sunaa and sukèè forms in Hausa (comparable to the Ibibio neutral and contrastive forms) is very obvious from Zima's observation (p. 191) below:

The basic facts remain the same: in the case of the sunàà/sukèè forms, which we shall simply call pair I forms, the alternation is almost fully predictable and automatic. If we schematically label all subordinate environments as b- environments and other environments (b excepted) as a − environments and call the forms subsequently A-form (sunàà) and B- forms (sukèè), we may define the alternation by a simple rule: within the pair I forms the A- forms must occur in a-environments and the B-form only in b-environments. Subsequently, there is no difference in meaning between the A-form and the B-form. A-form must automatically be replaced by b-form if we change the syntactic environment from a to b and vice-versa. The B-form is not allowed in a-environments and vice-versa.

This is exactly the case with the so-called neutral and contrastive allomorphs of the three tenses in Ibibio.

A similar conditioning of allomorphs or alternants has been observed in the tense / aspect system of Fululde (or Fula), an Atlantic language spoken in several West African countries, including Nigeria. This is reported by Zima (1986:587)

Essien (1991b) has reported many more similar cases from field investigations, in Nembe, an Ijoid language, Igbo, Ikom (sometimes known by the alternative name

Nkomej, an Upper Cross language, Kalabari, Igala, a Yoruboid language, etc. As observed by Essien (1991a:11), Zima (1988) and Hyman and Watters (1984) this seems to be an areal feature peculiar to Africa.

Comrie (1985:7) unaware of Zima's works nor mine, alludes to the existence of this phenomenon in Bantu languages in a foot-note in this way:

> In the grammar of some languages, moreover, the term tense has even a wider range of use. For example, many Bantu languages are described as having special `Tenses' for use in relative clauses and special negative tenses.

In the light of what we now know of the tendency in some languages for allomorphs of tenses (or tense/aspect) to alternate in accordance with the presence or absence of some categories like negation, Comrie's comment must be taken as a reflection of the syntactic conditioning of allomorphs of tense morphemes in negative, relative and many other constructions as high-lighted above. When, therefore, Hyman and Watters (1984:236) say that "it can thus be safely assumed that languages can have two sets of corresponding tense-aspect markers, one set occurring under focus the other not under focus" they are tacitly admitting syntactic conditioning of these tense – aspect markers.

What seems very clear whether from the auxiliary focus analysis or the syntactic conditioning analysis is that in many African languages, there are parallel tense/aspect markers which occur in certain mutually exclusive syntactic environments. In either analysis, these environments have been clearly identified and they are identical in both analyses. The simple Hausa rule given by Zima above suffices for most languages manifesting this phenomenon with equally simple modification to suit individual languages, while the Ibibio distributional equivalence is useful for languages with several or multiple alternants.

The major difference seems to be in the approach. Hyman and Watters seem to approach it from a semantic view point. For example, they talk of "the interaction between focus and the semantic features of tense, aspect, mood and polarity," while Essien and Zima clearly do so from the view point of the interplay between syntax and phonology, which is what make their analysis relevant to this conference.

4.7 Conclusion

Contrary to common assumption, we have shown that there is an interplay between phonology and syntax in a number of ways.

(i) From the organization of grammar proposed by generative grammarians of the Chomskyan tradition, the surface structure of a sentence generated by the syntactic component is the input to the phonological component. At the lexicon, itself part of the base subcomponent of the grammar, each lexical item is specified as a set of abstract morph-phonologoical and syntactic features. In any case the three components are integrated as part of UG.

(ii) While in a language like English, the phonetic form of a personal pronoun is determined by its function (such as subject, object, etc) in the sentence, in African languages tone, that is contrastive pitch, also commonly performs a grammatical or syntactic function, drawing phonology and syntax into a closer relationship.

(iii) But perhaps the most unusual case of the interplay between phonology and syntax is the intervention of syntax in the conditioning of tense/aspect phonetic forms in African languages. If the presence or absence of certain categories such as wh-question, negation, some form of emphasis or focus, some aspectual oppositions (depending on language), appear to influence the selection of the ultimate phonetic tense forms of a verb of many African languages, as we have demonstrated, then we maintain that there appears to be little doubt of the interaction of syntax and phonology in this aspect in such languages.

In our opinion, this is an important contribution of African languages to Linguistics, a contribution which goes beyond the Hyman and Watters auxiliary focus.

Chapter 5
Language, Literacy & Nation Building

5.1 Introduction

Language, literacy and nation building are interrelated, for one cannot think of a nation without a language nor can a nation be built without a written language. There has been no nation in history without a language with its own writing system. So language, literacy and nationhood had always been inseparable. Empires have come and gone, but those which have left their legacies have done so mostly through written records.

In this lecture, we propose to define these notions and examine the roles of language and literacy in the building or development of a nation. In particular we will draw attention to what appears to be a correlation between language and nation building or national development.

5.2.1 Language and its attributes

Language is one of the most intriguing phenomena in our universe. It is at once simple and complex, at once an individual and societal possession, at once limiting and creative, it can be both common and down-to-earth, and sublime and majestic. Intriguing, enigmatic, ordinary, vulgar (as English was once described), God's own gift, call language what you will, it resides in all of us and we are the custodian of it.

Because language resides in us and in communities as both personal and communal property, it is not difficult for people, linguist or not, to define it and at times for the non-linguist even to pontificate on it. Among the linguists there are many definitions which time will not permit us to go into. We will, therefore, do here what Essien (2003a) did by selecting a few of these definitions which seem to high-light some important aspects of language.

Sapir (1921:8), one of the two well-known American linguists who believed in linguistic relativism, defines language as, a "purely human and non-instinctive method of communication of ideas, emotions and desires by voluntarily produced symbols." This is one of the most frequently quoted definitions especially by people outside the discipline of linguistics. Yet, as observed by Lyons (1981:3-4), "it suffers from several defects. For example, a lot more is communicated than just ideas, emotions, and desires and this is why Essien (1983) has gone further to expound it in this way:

> Language is the thing with which we can best imagine, create, aspire, desire, feel and express our soul, enlarge our mental horizon and fulfill all that man is capable of.

Secondly, it does not say what kind of symbols are voluntarily produced- light, electromagnetic, sound, etc. Even voluntariness is open to question because there is

much else that is voluntarily and non-instinctively produced that we do not normally count as language that we all know and use. This includes gestures, postures, eye-gaze, whistling, coughing, etc.
(cf. Lyons 1981:3). Nor does it mention a very essential aspect of language, which Bloch and Trager (1942:5) do, namely: the relationship between the words of a language and their meaning.

However, it does include two essential aspects namely: it is limited to the human race or *homo sapiens* and it is used for communication, however inadequately communication may be viewed. In addition, no matter how much linguists disagree among themselves, the human language is infinitely and qualitatively less instinctive than animal communication systems.

A second popularly quoted definition – which I first heard myself as an undergraduate student of English – is Bloch and Trager's (1942:5) definition. Bloch and Trager define language as "a system of arbitrary vocal symbols by means of which a social group co-operate", Again, I begin by explaining what is wrong with this definition. I'm intrigued by what is meant by the expression **social group**. What does it really mean? For a social group refers to the vertical structure of the society – the upper (moneyed and leisurely) class, the middle class (or technocrats), the working class, etc. considering a highly stratified society like the United Kingdom. Does it mean that language is used for only intra-class or group communication? As far it is known linguistically, language is rooted in a community or society. From this point of view we have various linguistic (speech) communities like Hausa, Yoruba, Igbo, Ibibio, Edo, etc. communities. Within these communities, however, we do have social groups or classes which speak variations of the same language characterizing their respective community.

However, the definition advances Sapir's voluntarily produced symbols by stating that such symbols are vocal, i.e. sound, for there is no word without a sound (or sounds). We will return to this when we come to our own definition.

Noam Chomsky, the greatest and most influential linguist of our time, defines language in this way; "From now on I will consider a language to be a set of (finite or infinite) number of sentences, each finite in length and constructed out of a finite set of elements" (1957:13). This purely structural definition of language "says nothing about the communicative function of a natural or non-natural language; it says nothing about the symbolic nature of elements or sequences of them," as rightly observed by Sir John Lyons (1981:7). I can only say here that Chomsky is too intelligent to say simply what language is for the non-initiate.

In 1968, Chomsky together with Halle gave a better definition of language as follows:

We may think of a language as a set of sentences, each with an ideal phonetic form and an associated intrinsic semantic interpretation.

Although this definition includes a very important aspect of language, the sound or vocal aspect, it is still silent on the nature of the relationship between sound and meaning as well as on the communicative function of language.

Before we define language in our own way, let me amuse this distinguished audience somewhat with this ideologically feminist definition by Cameron (1990):

> Languages are cultural edifices whose norms are laid down in things like grammars, style books, and other glossaries- all of which have historically been compiled by men, and conservative men at that!

Male chauvinists, please hold on before you crucify Cameron. We don't have to go too far to illustrate the point of this definition, namely, that language is male-made. Or can you explain why Ibibio has a word primarily for a female prostitute -àkpàrà- but none for a male one (cf. Okon and Akpan 2001) and yet Ibibio men, like all men globally, are far more promiscuous than women. It does appear that as far as Ibibio men are concerned a man does not prostitute and therefore there is no need for a word for a concept that does not exist. Isn't this also true of men of other ethnic groups? Even from English, the dictionary definition of prostitute given by *Cambridge International Dictionary of English*, below:

> prostitute: a person, usually a woman, who has sex with someone else for money.

somewhat vindicates Cameron.

After that comic relief, let us define language as we see it.

> Language is a system of structural arbitrary vocal symbols by means of which human beings make meaning, communicate and interact with each other in a given community. Put more simply, Language is a system of rules and principles in which sound, structure and meaning are integrated for communication.

We explain a few key terms here. As a system, the components of language are ordered, not haphazard. Language is primarily vocal or spoken, but the sounds which it comprises must correspond to meaning, otherwise we would be making just noises, instead of talking language. This implies that our utterances must also be appropriate to the situation, otherwise communication breaks down. But the relationship between the sounds of a language as structured and what they mean or refer to in our real world is, for the most part, arbitrary. There is no logical or compelling reason why the particular sequence of sounds [o], [r] and [e] with a particular tonal melody (low-high) in the Yoruba word **òré** should mean `friend', anymore than the English people have a reason for calling what the Yoruba people call **òré friend** with its own particular sequence of sounds (or letters representing sounds). Sounds and their sequences in words, phrases and sentences simply arbitrarily refer to what they refer to, or mean what they mean in individual languages by convention. Of course there are onomatopoeic words and ideophones whose meanings seem to be related to, or can be determined by sounds. Onomatopoeic words include examples such as **bang, click,** etc in English. Ideophones include words such as **jim** in a number of Nigerian languages for the sound of a heavy falling object.

5.2.2 The biology and the power of language
Language is said to be "a species-specific human possession" because Chomsky (1981) and Lenneberg (1967) have postulated a biological basis for language acquisition insisting that there is an innate faculty of language or what Radford et al (1999) call acquisition programme in the brain making language acquisition and use possible. This, it is maintained emphatically, is specific to human beings but unavailable to any non-human animal including the most intelligent chimpanzee ever

found on the face of the earth. Chomsky, in particular, has progressed from characterizing this innate or biological endowment as incorporating a Language Acquisition Device (LAD) in the 1960s to Universal Grammar (or principles of UG in recent times).

Perhaps a brief description of the innate faculty of language is necessary at this point. This is not to imply that the direct study of the physical brain in relation to language is by any means easy. Biologists, anatomists and physiologists acknowledge that the brain is very complex. This brief summary paraphrased from Radford et al (1999:2) suffices for our purposes.

The brain consists of several `layers'. The layer which has evolved recently most characteristic of the higher primates like man is cerebral cortex, which is the folded surface of the cerebral hemisphere. These contain gray matter, the home of the higher intellectual functions including language. The cerebral cortex can be damaged in a number of ways. For example, it may suffer internal injury owing to disease or a blockage in a blood vessel resulting in disruption of the blood supply and death of cortical cells. Areas of damage are generally referred to as lesions.

The study of patients with various types of brain damage has revealed that different parts of the brain are associated with different functions. Some of these include problem solving, motor control and auditory processing. A large disorder resulting from the brain is referred to as aphasia. Need we be reminded that we must fasten our seat belt as we drive or are driven in a car, or wear a crash helmet when we ride a machine?

5.2.3 Language is power

This lecture would be incomplete if we fail to state one more important attribute of language, namely, that language is power.

If language is a cognitive system, biologically represented in the brain or mind, as stated above, and if the brain is the centre of man himself – or what is distinctively human, as some would say – then language, the very essence of man's humanity, is as essential and powerful as the very source of, it the brain.

It is language housed in the brain which provides man with the capacity for not only conceptualizing the world about himself but also for naming or tagging every concept in the universe, a job which was assigned to Adam according to Genesis 2:19-20, by God, thus making Adam the first ever linguist on earth (cf. Essien 2003a). This is a power or ability of enormous or stupendous proportion. Can anyone imagine a world of no language for we should remember that whether we are dreaming, praying or even reading silently, or writing or thinking or etc., we are doing so in a language? Language is immanent in all of us who have acquired it as a mother tongue or first language until we die when it departs from us. No wonder one Publius Syrus, according to Fry (1979) says: "Speech is a mirror of the soul: as a man speaks, so is he," and Chomsky (1972) from a mentalistic view point says "language is a mirror of the mind". We are indeed language or nothing.

So that is the power of language: it provides man with the capacity for conceptualizing the world and naming his mental concepts and is the mirror of his soul or mind. It is a gift of God and because of all these attributes, it rules the world. A country which toys with language, toys with what other wiser countries have done to become true nations.

5.3 Literacy

Literacy is concerned with the ability to read and write together with numeracy in a language. Therefore literacy is predicated on a language. There would be nothing to read or write or numeracy to use, if there were no language. Grudschinky (1976) taken from Stubbs (1980:13) describes a literate person in this more comprehensive way:

> That person is literate who, in a language, can read with understanding anything he would have understood if it had been spoken to him, and can write so that it can be read anything he can say.

A literate person is also expected to be cultured, widely read, tolerant and broad-minded. At the same time, the term illiterate is used also in everyday speech to refer, for example, to university students' essays which are badly spelled or stylistically poor" (Stubbs 1980:14).

5.3.1 Advantages of literacy

The advantages of literacy are so obvious that it would appear pointless restating them here. Still not all of them are patently obvious and we would like to consider them here, following Essien (2005a:19ff).

Firstly, although the primacy or priority of speech over writing is commonly recognized, especially among linguists, written language clearly serves different functions, which spoken language cannot, and therefore clearly augments speech.

For example, according to Stubbs (1980:15):

> Written material is used, for example, extensively in institutional and bureaucratic situations, for forms, notices, questionnaires, reports, letters and so on, where spoken language is never used.

So a people, whose language is unwritten and who are not literate in any other language are doomed in these areas. Similarly, if you cannot read and write, then the computer, the internet and information technology in general are of no use to you.

Secondly, according to Philips (1990:3):

> Literacy can provide a basis for economic, social and cultural development on a national and individual level. UNICEF research has shown that four years of schooling can change the pattern of a woman's life and increase her family survival from preventive health measure to family planning, to agricultural production.

As I write this lecture, the BBC is announcing the arrival of the dreaded bird flu in Nigeria. I shudder to think how our illiterate populations nation-wide are going to cope with this.

Thirdly, it is said (Stubbs 1980) that once a written language has come into a community, "it characteristically takes on something of a life of its own, and characteristically is regarded by its users as important and superior as a form of language." I think Ibibio people whose language was written more than two decades ago can testify to this. According to Stubbs (1980:30):

> There are some fairly obvious ways in which a written language has social priority over spoken language... In general, it is written forms of language which have social prestige... And it is written, often literary forms which are explicitly studied in our education system... In law, it is usually written forms which have precedence and

weight. Decisions may be required in writing and signatures may be required on written documents

And in addition, minutes of meetings are required to be written, not orally produced. In the case of minutes of an ethnic union, like the Ibibio Union in the 1930s, the minutes had to be produced in English for security reason. Perhaps this was also the case of other ethnic unions.

In this century, we need more than basic literacy. We need computer literacy. We have to be able to read and write cell phone and e-mail messages, have access to the internet and information technology in general. But all these are rooted in our primary ABC literacy and 123 numeracy, which we must maintain in order to be relevant in our fast-changing world.

For these reasons and others obvious enough, Essien (1983:3) appropriately describes the writing of a language for a community in this way.

> The writing of a language for the people who speak it must be one of the most important events in the history of such a people. Without a written language a people cannot preserve their history, their ethos, their philosophies, their heroic deeds and exploits, their myths and their legends.

That is why peoples whose languages are unwritten are said to be at a very low level of civilization and that is why farsighted people continue to work towards mass literacy, even if they do not achieve 100% success (cf. Bamgbose 2003:16).

It is not only the community that benefits from literacy: the individual in the community also does. By being able to read and write, he/she should also be able to communicate effectively, think critically and analytically in order to make his/her own contribution to the community in which he/she lives.

But commonly, a literate person is supposed to be cultivated, civil, tolerant, broadminded and respectful of the rights of others. One of the things an American is particularly good at is giving hospitality to foreign students, especially from third-world countries. Major American universities help newly arrived foreign students to get acquainted with the US through host families who can do so much to help sometimes, bewildered foreign students arriving in the US, for no gain whatsoever. Nor can you beat an American at helping people who need direction to get somewhere. I believe this is a function of the high literacy in that country.

On the other hand, there are certain behavioural traits that are viewed as unbecoming of literate people among the Ibibio people. If a man batters his wife, cannot live within his income, or is unable to educate his children properly, among other undesirable behavioural traits, a common remark is, "útọ́ ọ́wọ̀ òdò ọ́wọ̀t titia itìad-ñwed? "Has a man like that ever shown a slate to the teacher?"

That is, is someone like that literate? I believe this kind of expectation is not limited to the Ibibio, it is country-wide.

And this brings us to the crucial question? How many of us - graduates, civil servants, public servants, academics, politicians, professionals, etc do behave as truly literate and educated people and our communities judge us as such? Does literacy beget corruption?. This is a matter of conscience. But may it never be said of us by people in our community, "Did he show the teacher a slate?" So to build a nation, we require language and literacy, but this literacy must be reflected in our national ethos, values and integrity.

5.3.2 Literacy and micro-minor languages

Our thoughts on literacy would be deficient if we failed to address the issue in relation to what Bamgbose (1992) refers to as small group languages or Essien (2003b) as micro-minor languages.

Essien (2005a:18) gives characteristics of micro-minor languages in Nigeria, as follows:

(a) Numerically, by rule of thumb, they are spoken between three hundred thousand and five thousand people.

(b) They are least developed both in terms of corpus and status planning (i.e. in terms of basic development and in terms of recognition by government at any level).

(c) Their use is severely limited – generally confined to the home, local places of worship, village meetings, local burials, festivals and dances.

(d) They are rarely used on radio and television, except in strictly cultural programmes.

(e) They are found mostly in the South-South geo-political zone, the Middle Belt and other minority parts of the North.

(f) Speakers of these languages are by sheer necessity bilingual (in fact in some cases they speak more than two languages). In addition to their mother tongues, they must speak a major language: Hausa in the North and Yoruba in the West for sheer survival. Those in the East speak Igbo only if they were born and grew up in Igbo land, or lived in Rivers and Bayelsa States, which have a very strong Igbo presence. In Akwa Ibom State, Ibibio serves as a lingua franca for speakers of micro-minor languages, because these languages are genetically related to Ibibio. In Cross River, Rivers, Bayelsa, Edo and Delta States, the Nigerian Pidgin serves as a lingua franca for the many speakers of the micro-minor languages. So through these lingua francas, speakers of these micro-minor languages survive linguistically, even though many of them do not speak English.

(g) Over and above all the Nigerian languages (including the Nigerian Pidgin), speakers of micro-minor languages in Nigeria may speak English, if they go to School; Arabic, if they are Moslems; or French, if they studied this language in the university.

Although the micro-minor languages have little or no development, they form the majority of languages in Nigeria. Let us say in agreement with Bamgbose (1992) that there are four hundred languages in Nigeria. The six major languages – Hausa, Yoruba, Igbo, Ibibio, Kanuri and Fulfulde, so globally recognized (cf. Garry and Rubino 2001 and Essien 2003c) have basic developments and the first three a lot more. Languages such as Efik, Edo, Ijaw, Tiv, Nupe,. Idoma, Igala Berom, Kalabari, Ebira, Isoko, Kaye, Gbaye and Bwatye whose orthographies are found in the manuals of Nigerian Orthographies are being developed to enhance literacy in them. There are about two issues of the *Manual of Nigerian Orthographies* to which I have not yet had access. Presumably each contains about six orthographies of Nigerian languages. So altogether, then, thirty-four Nigerian languages of differing sizes have official orthographies. Allowing about twenty unofficial orthographies designed by Christian missionaries and some enterprising and far-sighted communities, following the Ibibio example in 1983, we can count about fifty mother tongues in Nigeria in which literacy is possible. That means about three hundred and fifty mother tongues in Nigeria have no orthographies or writing systems with which speakers of these languages can achieve literacy and be able to participate meaningfully in the building of their nation. And these languages are nearly all micro-minor languages. This, in our humble opinion, calls for a sober reflection and soul searching. But I am comforted by these brave words by the Father of Nigerian Linguistics, Professor Ayo Bamgbose:

> All those concerned with language issues must continue to aspire, for without aspiration and dreams no vision for the future can emerge (Bamgbose 2003:18)

5.3.4 Functional literacy

The most fundamental problem micro-minor languages face in the development of an orthography for each of them is their numerical strength. It is inconceivable to many people, particularly decision-makers, that the government should bother to cause such languages to be written. The number of speakers of such languages is not worth the labour and the expenses of devising and producing an orthography for each of them. Rather, they should accommodate themselves to the nearest major language or language of the immediate community with a standard orthography (cf. Jibril 1990:116).

Considering Bamgbose's (2003:18) advice or realism, we would like to recommend functional literacy for such linguistic communities in the interest of the nation at large.

According to Stubbs (1980:14), the term functional literacy has been introduced by Gray (1956) to describe the UNESCO – organized literacy programmes for the third-world countries. Literacy is defined in this connection relative to the needs of an individual and a particular community or society. It is the degree or extent of literacy required for effective functioning in a particular community or society. For example, the literacy needs of a Brazilian peasant are different from those of an American Urban dweller, according to Stubbs (1980). In this way the literacy needs of the speakers of the major languages of Nigeria are unlikely to be the same as those of the speakers of micro-minor languages. For example, Yoruba is an internet language but clearly that is not what Okobo, spoken by not more than ninety thousand people in Akwa Ibom State needs: it needs the more basic aspects of language development that will enable a rural Okobo woman to have at least four years of schooling so that her rural life may be qualitatively changed according to the UNCESCO research reported above.

In particular Essien (2005:22) lists the following basic things that functional literacy should enable such rural people to do:

- Write down the name, sex, date, and place of birth of their children.

- Keep a record of landed property, cattle, sheep, goats, fowls, debts/debtors, creditors, etc.
- Keep account of sales from whatever goods/services are available in a rural setting.
- Read the Bible or whatever holy writings are available in their local language.
- Keep a record of useful plants/herbs for medicinal purposes in the local language.
- Record names of people, events and places one is likely to forget as well as addresses of people one is likely to relate with.
- Read road signs, bill boards, posters, etc. in the local language, especially on HIV/AIDS and other killer diseases and on one's civic responsibilities
- Be able to read and write folk tales in one's language and be curious about one's people and their past.

In this way functional literacy will go a long way towards integrating rural communities with government at the grassroots and even beyond.

5.4 **Nation building**
And now we come to the third component of our lecture. One of my GSS lecturers at Nsukka in the 1960s clearly asserted that Nigeria was a country, not a nation. He must have meant by this what Chief Awolowo meant by Nigeria

being a mere "geographical expression," according to Agi (1999:114).

At forty-five now, are we now a nation? Political scientists say defining a nation is far from easy. However, Emerson (1962) according to Agi (1999:110) defines the term in this way:

> The nation is a community of people who feel that they belong together in the double sense that they share deeply significant elements of a common heritage and that they have a common destiny.

This feeling of belonging together arising from shared deep significant elements and a common heritage and having a common destiny for the future distinguishes a nation from a nation-state. Nigerians in the 1960s cannot be blamed for not thinking of their state as a nation and it is a moot point how many of them really do so over thirty years later.

But what needs to be done to build Nigeria as a nation? Economists and political scientists have made suggestions. For example, the latter (cf. Agi 1999:112-113) give factors from a political view which are quite useful for nation building but he didn't say anything about the role of language and literacy. Economically, the government has presented a reforms agenda, which Essien (2005a) critically examined and need not be repeated here. As in the political agenda, no mention was made of the role of language.

The much attention given to language in this lecture is informed by the failure of economists, politicians, government advisers and technocrats, and above all decision makers in government circles to recognize the role of language in nation building or national development, a matter which Essien has given considerable attention for some years now (cf. Essien 1977, 2003b, 2005a, 2005b). In view of time constraint, I will select just a few of the highlights of these papers to conclude this lecture.

In 1977, we said this:

> If we want great thinkers, we must give those gifted in thinking adequate language. If we want great artists – poets, playwrights, novelists, musicians, etc, we must make it possible for such talented people to acquire such facility in language as will enable them to express their imagination, feelings and insight freely. If we want great scientists and inventors, language must not inhibit those who have the innate abilities. If we want great politicians, economists, historians, linguists, etc language should not stifle those who are gifted (Essien 1977).

But the power of language is limited unless one knows it well as a mother tongue or first language.

In 2003, we also said this:

> In so far as man is inseparably *homo sapiens* and *homo-loquens*, insofar as education, a vital ingredient in development, is inconceivable without language and insofar all notions, concepts, theories, arguments, analyses and practices in all academic disciplines that enhance national development [or nation building] find expression in languages..., the role of language in the national development enterprise cannot be over-emphasized. (Essien 2003b:25)

This shows the indispensability of language in national development. Again this is applicable to the mother tongue or the language the nation knows very well.

In 2005, we discussed literacy, including literacy in the micro-minor languages, and its advantages and functions. Literacy and language are inseparable and there is no nation without a written language. (cf. Essien 2005a)

Still in that same year, we made the following observations, which should be instructive to those aspiring to build a nation.

> As each new nation was born, an official language was also born. Such a language (or languages)

became a basic expression of identity and aspiration. Governments of such new nations responded by embarking on planning, that is "... a government authorized long term, sustained and conscious effort to alter a language," according to Weistein (1980:56). It is quite clear that nationhood, economic, legal, socio-cultural and **linguistic** developments were integrated in European nations. The new nations (e.g. Denmark, Sweden, Czech Republic, etc.) followed in the footstep of the older nations like France, Italy, Britain, Germany, etc. No wonder, then, European nations, old or new are where they are – far above the new Black African nations whose developments take no cognizance of the enormous potential of language. When Allen (1976) says that he who controls language, controls history, he or she is partially right. We should say that he who controls language controls history and destiny... Although records of what the Japanese and Chinese did to their respective languages are not available to us, we have little doubt that they must have done essentially what the Europeans did to their respective languages. In any case, as far as we know, the Japanese language and the Chinese language have always been used by the Japanese and Chinese respectively for all forms of communication. The Asian `Tigers' like South Korea,

Taiwan, Thailand, India, Indonesia, etc have recognized indigenous languages as indispensable tools in nation building or national development. Language, in our view, may therefore be Meier's (1976) "unidentified residual factor" in development.

There is, therefore, ample evidence from those nations which have already developed and those which are nearly developed that language, "the human essence", "this quintessence of humanity" is a latent source of power, imagination, creativity, thought, dream and vision behind every nation building or national development. We are therefore impelled to repeat what we suggested last year (cf. Essien 2005b): Nigeria must learn from others who have built or developed their nations and initiate a national agenda for linguistic reforms in line with other national reforms agendas, for it appears from history that there is a correlation between language and nation building.

Chapter 6
Introduction to African Linguistics
(A USP Lecture)

6.1 Introduction

Perhaps we should begin this course with what we all know: the definition of linguistics. I have found the definition of this term by Lyons (1968) to be very useful and I repeat it here for you.

> Linguistics is the scientific study of language as an entity through an objective and rigorous description and analysis. It is a science because work on language is done by means of controlled and empirically verifiable observations and with reference to some theory of language structure

Such a theory may be the structuralist theory of American Linguistics of the 1940s and 1950s, Firth's prosodic phonology of Great Britain, Halliday's Scale and Category or Functional grammar, Lamb's Stratificational grammar, Chomsky's government and binding theory or the most recent minimalist theory of his.

For the chemist, element and their reactions constitute his domain of investigation and study, for the physicist, it is matter and energy, while for the biologist, it is living things. For the linguist, then, language is his field of investigation and he approaches it with the same controlled and empirically verifiable observation, the same objectivity, the same detachment, the same vigour and the same exhaustiveness that characterize the physical sciences.

It is not surprising, therefore, that Caroll (1953) according to Newmeyer (1981:1) has described the discipline of linguistics as the most advanced of all the social sciences with close resemblance to physics and chemistry. In an even more flattering term, Levi-Strauss (1953:250-51) has compared the discovery that language consists of phonemes and morphemes to the Newtonian revolution in physics.

In the best tradition of Science (cf. Essien 2003) quite often linguists from different countries (and even continents) working independently on totally different language data come to the same or similar conclusions. A classic example of relevance to African Linguistics involves a certain phenomenon in Ibibio, a Niger- Congo language and Hausa, a Chadic language – indeed two very genetically different languages. For some years one Professor Peter Zima, a linguist from the Czech Republic in Eastern Europe and I had been working independently and unknown to each other on Hausa and Ibibio, respectively. In the 1990s, however, through our individual publications, we discovered, to our amazement and delight that our independent analyses of the data in Hausa and Ibibio, respectively, have come to the same conclusion. That's how scientific linguistics can be even with data from African languages. According to Clements (2000:124)," New data from Africa has provided a corrective to the often Eurocentric bias of earlier linguistic theories, and has stimulated many recent developments in linguistic theory" Although linguistics is a science, it is the most humanistic of all the sciences.

6.2 Justification of African linguistics

One may wonder, why African Linguistics? Do we have different kinds of *Linguisticses*? Yes indeed we already do so: We have general linguistics, historical linguistics, etc. In each of these kinds of linguistics, there is sufficient body of knowledge of special kind (or body of specialist knowledge) to justify their being called or referred to so. And even more importantly, such specialist divisions enhance research into and acquisition of more specialist bodies of knowledge in these areas. Similarly there is sufficient specialist knowledge or body of specialist knowledge on Linguistic material and research on language in the US to warrant a peculiarly American linguistic content to be referred to as American Linguistics. This is true of British, Canadian, Brazillian, Japanese, Portuguese, etc., Linguistics for decades now, there has been a growing and exciting body of knowledge of African languages genetically, typological, areally, phonologically, morphologically, sociolinguistically, etc., to warrant the nomenclature African Linguistics. This speciality, as in the case of other specialities, enables scholars and lovers of knowledge to investigate, describe and analyse the languages of what has often been described by Europeans as a 'terra incognita', and thereby gain wider insights into human or natural language, the unique possession of homo sapiens. We therefore have no apologies for the specialty African Linguistics.

6.3 The beginnings of African linguistics

What is now African Linguistics can be said to have had its very beginning in the 17th Century. According to Clements (2000:123), "the linguistics study of African languages dates back to Fr. Giancinto Bisciotto's grammar of the Bantu language Kongo (Kikongo), published in Rome". But the study of African languages began in earnest in the 19th Century under the influence of Indo-European comparative-historical studies arising from the discovery of works on Sanskrit by Panini. From the scholarly impetus of comparative historical scholars works such as the following in Bantu Languages began to appear before the 20th century and early in the 20th century:

'Das Verbum in der Isubu. Spache' by C. Meinhof, ZAS, 1889, Grammar of the Benga-Bantu Language by R. H. Nassau, 1892, Heads of Mpongwe Grammar, 1879, 'Grammatik des Duala' by J. Ittman 1914, 'Grammatik de Nkosi-Sprache' with 'Vocabularium der Nkosi-Sprache by E. Dorsch, in Z.F.K.S., 1911, all of which are taken from Malcom Guthrie (1953). But by that year Guthrie was able to compile a publication entitled *Handbook of African Languages: The Bantu Languages of Western Equatorial Africa* as a professor of Bantu Languages, University of London. In addition, there were later grammatical works in other Bantu languages like Swahili, Bantu languages being the best known and most exciting languages. In West Africa, Hausa, one of the major languages of Nigeria, had received attention while surprisingly as early as 1875, Rev. J.G. Christeller of the Basel German Evangelical Mission had published a highly acclaimed book entitled *A Grammar of the Asante and Fante Language.* Thirteen years earlier in 1862, Rev. Hugh Goldie had published another highly rated linguistic work entitled, *Dictionary of the Efik Language* in 1862 (Glasgrow) and another one entitled Principles of Efik Grammar, with specimens of the language in 1868 (Edinburgh). These and many other later works on African languages were inspired by European Christian Missions to envangelise the African Continent.

However, according to Clements (2000:123) the scientific study of African languages received a major impetus in the first part of the twentieth century from the enormous amount of descriptive works carried out by linguists based in Africa, Europe and North America. In all these efforts primary attention was given to phonology. In recent times, the description and analysis of African languages have been enhanced and strengthened by advances in linguistic theory. In particular Chomsky's generative grammar in both phonology and syntax and its various offshoots have significantly influenced the "examination of African languages in order to obtain understanding of universal properties of human language faculty itself. "And recent works on tense, aspect, moved (or what is referred to as TAM by Creissels 2000:239) by scholars like Lyons (1977) and Comrie (1976, 1985) have facilitated the descriptions and analyses of many African languages, certainly superior to the lumping of the tense, aspect and modal markers together under the very uninsightful analysis of Welmers's construction markers (cf. Welmers 1973).

6.4 The objective of the course

Our basic assumption is that the students at the beginning of their graduate work in the Department of Linguistics are going to be introduced to African Linguistics for the first time. In other words, they have had little or no acquaintance with African Linguistics. If some of the lectures are going to be already familiar with it, I'm awfully sorry. This is because we wish to accommodate everybody, a majority of whom, I understand, are unfamiliar with African Linguistics. For those who have already had some familiarity, may I say as I would in Nigeria, bear with me.

The course, then, aims at introducing African Linguistics in order to broaden the scope of the students' knowledge of linguistics as an academic discipline which is both scientific and humanistic. African Linguistics is linguistics with African languages as the focus on the core levels of language structure- phonology, morphology, syntax and semantics as well as the non-core areas of sociolinguistics, historical/comparative linguistics, history, ethnology and naming as both a linguistic and cultural enterprise. The course will also include language typology and areal classification as they affect African languages.

Until very recently – thanks to Chomsky's untiring efforts in the search for universals of language as a strictly human possession, some American Africanists have tended to make veiled derogatory statements about African languages. For example, Welmers (1973:vii), a well-known American Africanists, has said this:

> It is the purpose of this work to survey a variety of structural phenomena which appear commonly in African languages... but which are not necessarily typical of human languages in the broadest sense.

Consciously or unconsciously Welmers appears to be questioning the status of African languages here as proper human languages, because of structural differences from typical European languages, differences which are best linguistically – and therefore scientifically – viewed as parametric differences. It is hoped that the Brazillian students of linguistics will have a more balanced view of African Languages through this course.

6.5 Structural characteristics of African languages

Let us now begin to examine some of those structural features which appear to be peculiar to African languages, phonologically, morphologically, and syntactically. We will consider ideophones as we examine morphology, since they are words.

6.5.1 Phonology

In considering phonology, we will look at both the traditional segments and non-segments variously referred to in the literature as prosodic, suprasegmental or autosegmental.

6.5.1.1 Common phonemes/segmental units of African languages

Clements (2000:125) gives a table of what he terms 'a "protypical" African phoneme system below:

p	t	c	k		i		u
b	d	ɟ	g		e		o
m	n	ɲ	ʔ		ɛ		ɔ
f	s	ʃ	h			a	
	z						
	l						
w	r	y					

where /c/ represents any voiceless postalveolar stops and affricates, /ʃ/ any postalveolar fricative, and /r/ any rhotic

Vital Aspects of Linguistics 137

('r-sound'). Some African languages, however, like Ibibio, a Niger-Congo language, has 'exotic' central vowels like /ə, ʌ/ (as Clements would choose to describe them). Ibibio also has diphthongs, which are considered rare in African vowel systems.

Then he (Clements) goes on to identify what he describes as 'phoneme types commoner in Africa than elsewhere and these are:

Implosives like /ɓ/, /ɗ/ as in Hausa ɗaya: 'one'; labio-velar stops like /kp/, /gb/ as in Kalabari (Nig. Con) Kpákpō: 'hook'; initial consonant clusters (NC) as in Igbo, Niger-Congo ǹdó 'sorry'; clicks, rather difficult sounds found in Khoisan languages. Outside Khoisan languages, clicks are known to occur only in South Bantu languages such as Zulu, Xhosa, Southern Sotho and Yeyi, and in the Cushitic language, Dahalo/. Lower high vowels /ɪ, ʉ/ occur in Ibibio and Igbo, Niger-Congo languages.

Let us now go into some details of these more commonly occurring sounds in African Languages:

6.5.1.1.1 Implosives

Because I know Portuguese does not have this sound and you are unlikely to be familiar with it, I would like to describe it here for you as done by Ladefoged (1975:122), a former professor of mine.

It is also possible to use a downward movement of the larynx to suck air inward. Stops made with an ingressive glottalic airstream mechanism are called implosives. In the production of implosives, the downward moving larynx is not usually completely closed. The air in the lungs is still being pushed out, and some of it passes between the cords, keeping them in notion so that the sound is voiced.

All implosives are then voiced. It is not surprising, therefore, that in African languages, implosives pattern with sonorant consonants such as liquids, glides and nasals in many respects. So for implosives, as for these three categories of consonant sounds, voicing is unmarked. Like sonorants also, implosives are fully nasalized in the context of nasalized vowels, as in the case in Ebrié, a Niger-Congo language in West Africa, do not occur in Nasal + Consonant or C+ Nasal cluster and often occur in complementary distribution with sonorant consonants. Thus, according to Clements (2000:132), /l/ is realized as /ɗ/ before high vowels or glides in Ebrié referred to above. The patterning or behaviour of implosives in African languages suggests strongly, according to Clements (ibid), that such implosives are not obstruents after all, but in fact sonorants after which they pattern. In this way implosives satisfy Halle (1992:208)'s definition of sonorant sounds as "sounds produced without a pressure build-up inside the vocal tract; non-sonorant sounds are produced with pressure in the vocal tract that exceeds the ambient atmospheric pressure" (cf. Clements ibid). This is a very clear instance of the contributions to Linguistics by African languages. Below are a few examples of words containing implosives in Uduk, a Nilo-Saharan language taken from Ladefoged (1975:123)

(1) a. ɓal: 'back of neck'
     b. ɗek: 'to lift'
     c. deɗ: 'to shiver'
     d. t'ɗ: 'lick'

Incidentally sounds such as /k'/ and /t'/ are ejectives, which also occur in some African languages such as Hausa, a Chadic language, but not confined to African languages.

6.5.1.1.2 Labio-velar stops (or doubly articulated stops)

In the production of some sounds in African language, two places of articulation are involved, even though the complex sounds are regarded as unit sounds. This state of affairs is not peculiar to African languages. The English sounds ch [tʃ] and j [dʒ] in the English words: chin [tʃɪn] and jump [dʒʌmp] are two good examples from a European language. In the production of some stops, the lips and the back of the tongue (velum) are involved. Such sounds are called labial velars or labio-velars. Many West African languages such as Ewe a Kwa Niger-Congo language spoken in Ghana, and Yoruba, another Niger-Congo spoken as one of the three major languages of Nigeria, have the labio-velar stops /kp/ and /gb/. Consider the following Yoruba examples

(2) a. akpá: 'arm'
    b. agba: 'old'

There could also be a nasal counterpart of /gb/, namely /ŋm/. It is possible for an African language to have the ordinary stops (voiced and voiceless) implosives and doubly articulated stops as given for Kalabari Ijo below by Clements (2000:129)

Voiceless (explosive) stops:
   p   t   k   kp   kw

Voiced (explosive) stops:
   b   d   dʒ   g   gb   gw

Voiced implosive stops
   ɓ   ɗ

The major places of articulation reviewed above are often supplemented by secondary articulation such as labialization, Cʷ, Palatalization, Cʸ, Velarization C or Uvularization (as in Berber and Arabic). In the case of labialization, this often arises historically in the context of [u] or [w] while palatalzation arises in the context of (i) and [y]. There are controversies arising from the analysis of a phonetic kw- as /ku/ or /kw/ or even as labialized /kʷ/. In my analysis of Ibibio, I have argued for a /ku/ analysis.

6.5.1.1.3 Initial nasal consonant clusters NC

Perhaps we ought to consider consonant clustering in general in African languages. Although my view of consonant clustering is different from Clements's, to minimize unnecessary argumentation, I will go along with his definition of it as "any phonetic sequence of consonants without prejudice as their eventual analysis as one or two phonemes".

Consonant clustering is not a pronounced feature of African languages, especially at the phonemic level, certainly not comparable to the English language where it is possible to have three consonants clustering in one syllable whether as onset or coda (**street** or **punks**). That's why words such as **scoop, school** present learning problems to some African learners like the Hausa speaking people of Northern Nigeria. However, many African languages do have consonant clustering of some sort. But such clusters do raise difficult problems of analysis. In some cases, they can be shown to behave as single, phonetically complex sounds while in others they behave as phonemic sequences. A satisfactory analysis often depends on how a given cluster is syllabified.

According to Clements (2000:145) consonant clusters generally lend themselves to one of the four possibilities given below:

4)

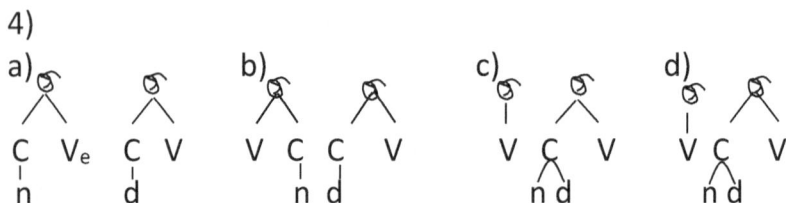

As explained by Clements (ibid), in (4a) the cluster is analysed as a sequence of two onsets separated by a phonologically 'empty' (symbolized by e) syllable peak (V_e), in (4b) as a coda + onset sequence, in (4c) as a complex onset consisting of two phonemes and in (4d) as a simple onset consisting of one phoneme, whose features are sequenced only at the phonetic level.

Clusters often involve the following

(i) Cy or Cw, i.e. Consonant plus an approximant, where phonetically it is perceived as ci and cu, respectively but phonemically as Cy or Cw, (cf Welmers 1974) respectively.

(ii) *Liquid Clusters:*
Many West African languages have liquid clusters CL, where L is realized as [l] or [r]. Often there arise historically from the deletion of a vowel. Ibibio, a Niger-Congo language and the fourth largest language of Nigeria presents an

interesting case. Consider the following examples (cf. Essien 1990):

(5) a. trĕ (from tịdé) : 'stop'
    b. frĕ (from fịdé) 'forget'
    c. bré (From bịdé) 'be dark in complexion

To derive **trĕ**, **frĕ** and **bré** from **tịde**, **fịdé** and **bịdé** respectively requires the deletion of the **ị** and the wakening of the /d/ to [r] (actually [ɾ]) (cf. Essien 1990). Observe that the post - liquid vowel [ĕ] in (5a) and (5b) bears the tone of the deleted short vowel [ɨ], hence the contour tone on it, Similar analysis is applicable to CLV (from CVLV) synchronic syllabic structure of many West African Languages.

(iii) *Nasal Clusters NC.* Welmers (1973:65ff) has asked pertinent questions about possible interpretations of nasal + consonant sequences. Are they to be taken as unit phonemes or as clusters? And if they are clusters, are the nasal components non-syllabic or syllabic?]

According to him; "all possibilities and some combinations of possibilities occur." In some languages, like Efik, Ibibio and Igbo, all of which are Niger-Congo languages, the nasal is always syllabic and such clusters may occur only initially, in these languages the nasal is always homorgamic with the following consonant, oral or nasal. In Ibibio, Essien (1990:19) analyses the syllabic nasals as allophones of /n/. The syllabic nasals generally perform a morphological function.

As shown earlier (see example (4a) Clements (2000: 145) suggests that some instances of NC is analyzable as NV_eC, where the V_e has been deleted.
Here are some instances of syllabic nasal + consonant

(6) a. m -o b aɨke Brazil
       1st sg-be in Brazil = I'm in Brazil
    b. ń - tiè o mi
       1st sg - sit here=   'I'm sitting down here
    c. ŋ - kà Ùdùà
       1st sg - go market = I'm going to the Market'

In Akan, a Niger-Congo language of Ghana, initial nasals before consonants are also syllabic, as observed by Welmers (though there are said to be non-initial syllabic nasals)

(7) a. ḿpá: 'mat'
    b. n-tém: 'haste'
    c. ŋ-gʊ́: 'oil'

As shown earlier (see example 4 above), Clements (2000:145) suggests that some instances of NC is analyzable as NV_eC, where the V_e has been deleted to bring it to NC. In other languages, the entire sequence belongs to one syllable with the following vowel. Welmers

(1973:66) gives the following examples from Jukun (Benue-Congo, Northern Nigeria.

(8) [mbù]: /mù/:   'white'
     [nde]: /né/   'noise'
     [ŋga]:   'try'

According to Welmers's analysis, [mb, nd, ng] are allophones of the /m, n, ŋ/ nasal phonemes.

Perhaps we ought to make one small point in passing in regard to homorganic assimilation. This is found in languages outside Africa such as Indonisian (cf. Clark & Yallop 1990:142-3) with such sequences as /mb/ and /nd/ while in English the /n/ of the negative prefix /in-/ is homorganic with the following oral consonant, as the following examples show:

(9) a Impossible   [ɪmposəbl]
       Indecent   [ɪndi:snt]
       Incorrect   [ɪŋkərekt]

(iv)   *Clicks*

Nearly all authors agree that clicks are uncommon phonetic sounds. According to Clark and Yallop (1990:58) clicks are found in rather few languages forming about 1% of the world's languages (according to Maddieson (1986). They are characteristic of the Khoisan languages of the Kalahari area of South Africa and some parts of East Africa, as we shall see later. Although there are non-linguistic clicks (e.g. some kind of gentle kissing sound, interjection expressing disapproval or the noise used to signal horses, clicks as human speech sounds are not known outside of a small area of southern Africa and East Africa.

Ladefoged (1975:123) describes the production of clicks as having the mouth air rarefied by the backward and downward movement of the tongue. The source of air stream is velaric and the direction of the air is ingressive. The air trapped between the front of the mouth with the lips or tongue front, and another in the back of the mouth is expanded by drawing the tongue body downward and backward while maintaining both closieres, and the front closure is then released to produce a click as air rushes into the moth. Clicks can be represented as follows:

(10)a. ʃ   dental click   e.g. ʃaʃa   'climb'
    b. b   alveolar lateral click e.g. boba
    c. c   post alveolar click e.g. caca: 'explain'

6.5.1.1.4 Systems and vowel processes

We have already looked at homorganic assimilation in relation to NC above. The following vowel systems and sometimes variants, are found widely in African Languages.

(ii) (a)

```
    i     u        i     u        i     u
    e     o        e     o        ɨ     ʉ
       a              ɛ     ɔ        e     o
                         a              ɛ     ɔ
                                           a
```

All these systems have a symmetrical set of front and back vowels and an additional non-low central /a/. Variants of these systems with an additional non-low central vowel /ə/ are also not uncommon. Ibibio, a Niger-Congo Nigerian language has a system with /ə/ and non-low /ʌ/, as given below:

Ibibio vowel system
(12)

```
            i           u
            ɨ           ʉ
         e     ə     o
               ʌ     ɔ
                  a
```

This is something that eluded Kaufman (1968) who gave Ibibio an outrageously misleading five vowel system, when the language is known to generously provide minimal pairs (cf. Essien 1990) and even what Essien (1987) refers to as "minimal trio".

Of the vowel processes, one seems to be more common in some African languages than languages elsewhere. This is vowel harmony.

6.5.1.1.4.1 **Vowel harmony**

Essien (1990:41) defines vowel harmony as:

> A process by which the vowels of a language, usually in a single word, are so constrained that all of them must have some property or properties in common as determined by the phonological environment.

In that publication, Essien took an issue with the definition given below by Williamson (1984:70), a definition which is favoured by many other linguists working on African languages such as Stewart (1967), Welmers (1973), Clements 1985), etc.

> The system whereby in many languages, the vowels are divided into two sets, 'wide' and 'narrow' in such a way that vowels from the same set normally go together in some simple word.

According to Essien (ibid), by this Williamson and others like her appear to view vowel harmony only from one set of phonetic features – tongue root advancement versus tongue not retraction. Admittedly the tongue root advancement/retraction parameter, by which Igbo, Akan, Kalabari, etc., vowels are selected in a word gives a perfect and more straightforward type of vowel harmony. But clearly this must be viewed as one example of the process, in our opinion. Indeed Hyman (1975:233-235) gives several typologies of vowel harmony. According to him,

> While complete vowel harmony is often referred to as vowel copying or vowel reduplication, most cases referred to as vowel harmony are of partial variety. In this case a vowel assimilates in certain features to another vowel. The most essential features assimilated are front-backness, tense-laxness and labiality.

The terms used in the literature to describe vowel harmony in many West African languages such as the Igbo, Akan and Kalabari are the following pairs of terms: 'wide' versus 'narrow', 'tense' versus 'lax' and 'advanced tongue root' versus 'retracted tongue root. This last pair of terms is now commonly referred to as +ATR or -ATR. In the Akan language of Ghana, for the sake of vowel harmony, the vowels of the language are divided into two sets as follows:

(13) a. [+ATR]   b   [-ATR]
         /i, e, u, o/   /ɪ, ɛ, ʉ, ɔ, a/

In Igbo, one of the four major languages of Nigeria, the harmonic sets are paired as follows

(14) a. [+ATR]   b   [-ATR]
         /i, e, o, u/   /ɨ, ʉ, ɔ, a/

In keeping with the harmony principle based on [±ATR], in Igbo, for example, vowels do not criss-cross in a word. If the vowel of the root of a word occurs from a [+ATR] set, then it automatically selects another vowel from the [-ATR] set in the affix, as given in (14a). Thus there are Igbo words such as (15) and not (16) below.

(15) a. égȯ: 'money'
        b. ʊlɔ: 'house'

(16) a   *iha
        b   *ake

Besides the [±ATR] harmony principle, the front-back parameter is also found in many African Languages. The Efik-Ibibio-Annang cluster of very closely related Niger-Congo languages, offers a good example. The examples in Ibibio in (17) below illustrate our point.

(17) a. díppé: 'lift up'
        b. dóppó : 'be heavy'
        c. dakka: 'go away'

This kind of harmony often results in vowel copying as the (b) and (c) examples show, especially where the root has a non-high vowel. Since front rounded vowels are rare, if existent at all in African languages, and back vowels are predictably [+ round], [± round] also features as part of the harmonic principle in such cases. This is similar, though to vowel harmony in Turkish.

6.5.1.2 Prosodic system and tone

As it is commonly known, most African languages are tonal, though in Nigeria one language, Fulfulde or Fula is non-tonal. Tone is defined as contrastive pitch by which the differences in relative pitch are used to convey differences in lexical meaning and grammatical function. Pitch itself is caused by the vibration of the vocal cords or bands and by pitch contrast is meant the changes or variations in the pitch level affects the meaning of a word and the grammatical function of its constituent parts. Consider the following examples taken from Ibibio.

(18) a. wák: 'be many'
       b. wàk: 'tear into pieces

where the difference in meaning arises from the pitch level: (18a) is said with a high pitch while (18b) is said with a low pitch. It is such contrastive pitches that are referred to as tones. Tones are as much a part of the lexical item as consonants and vowels are. For Goldsmith (1979), then, tones are as segmental as consonants and vowels, the traditional segments, hence his autosegmental phonology. Tone systems are also found outside Africa, China in particular. But the African tonal system is different from the Chinese type, which is a contour system, while the

African tone system is register, in which the tones have discrete level pitches with no glide while the Chinese system is made up of contour tones with gliding pitches.

The African register system, the commonest of which is found in Niger-Congo and Nilo-Sharan languages, usually comprises two distinctive tone levels, high (H) and low (L) but often allows two or more of these tones in a succession on single syllables, thus creating what are often commonly referred to as contour tones. Let me be quick to point out that such contours are easily dissolved into a high-low contour, in the case of a falling contour tone, or a low-high contour tone, in the case of a rising tone. According to Clements (2000:152), in Mende, for example, there are five contrastive tone patterns on monosyllabic nouns alone, as the following examples show:

19)(a) kɔ: 'war' (H);   (b) kpà: 'debt' (L);
　　(c) mbû: 'owl' (HL);   (d) mbǎ : 'rice' (LH),
　　(e) mbã̌: 'companion (LHL).

In some languages, like Nupe, a Niger-Congo language spoken in Northern Nigeria, there is a third level tone, the mid tone, while in Ibibio, there is a downstepped tone, analysed as a slightly lowered high tone, historically. Essien (2005) has, however, reanalysed it as a mid tone.

As remarked by Clements (ibid), perhaps the most outstanding feature of tones in African languages is their independence of their segmental support. Tones appear to behave as if they exist on a separate tier from consonants and vowels, given the following characteristics, listed by Clements (2000:153).

(a) *Tone melodies.* Significant sequences can often be stated over tone sequences (melodies) in abstraction from the segments that bear them.

(b) *Contour tones.* Rising and falling tones can usually be analyzed as combinations of two or more level tones (H, L etc) as already pointed out above).

(c) *Spreading tones.* Single level tones may spread over several syllables at once.

(d) *Floating tones.* Some tones float between other tones, often causing the raising of the preceding tone, or lowering (down step) of following tones.

(e) *Tone shift.* Tones charactering one morpheme can be realized on other morpheme, sometimes at a considerable distance away.

These properties are explained insightfully by Goldsmith's theory of Autosegmental phonology (cf. Goldsmith 1976 and 1990). The basic premise of autosegmental tonology is that tones are represented on a tie of their own paralleling that of consonants or vowels and are synchronized or associated with units that bear them by means of association lines given below, taking examples from Igbo:

(19) H L
   (a)   ulɔ 'house'

   (b)   after association
```
         H L           H
         | |           /\
         ul ɔ         anya
         'house'      'eye'
```

Tones can also perform grammatical functions such as those of person, aspect, mood, etc. For example in Ibibio, the difference between the second and third person concord markers or dependent pronouns is signalled by tone, as the following examples show.

(20) a. àmààká:
            2npsg past go   = you (sg) went
      b. ámáàkă: = he (she) it went

where **à** and **á** with a low tone and high tone on the vowel **a** indicates 2nd person singular and 3rd person singular respectively. Similarly, the different tonal melodies on the future markers -yàá - and yàá - indicate indefinite and immediate future respectively in the following examples:

(21)   ń-yàá -dí
       1st Psg-fut-come
       'I will come' (in some indefinite future)

   ń-yáá -dí
   1st Psg-fut-come
   'I will come' (very soon, almost immediately)

6.5.1.2.1 Tonal phenomena
There are many tonal phenomena. But in this introductory course, we will limit ourselves to three very important ones, which do not necessarily occur in all tone languages of Africa.

6.5.1.2.1.1 Downdrift and downstep
Confusion often arises in the use of the term downstep (or downstepping). For this reason, let us distinguish between the terms downstep and downdrift (or downstepping and downdrifting).

It has been observed that in many African languages like Akan, Igbo, Hausa, Ibibio, etc. the pitch register drops in absolute value as the phrase is articulated. This declination or drop is referred to as downdrift or downstep, depending on how it occurs and its function. Downdrift takes a number of forms. However, a common form of downdrift realizes a string of high-toned syllables after a low-tone syllable at a slightly lower pitch value than the preceding high. That is, each successive high tone in a

HLHLHLH sequence, for example, is articulated at a slightly lower value than the preceding high, tone after a low tone. In some languages, the low tone also drops in value but in others, it doesn't. This is both tonal and intonational, affecting both polysyllabic words and phrases, as in the following example taken from Ibibio

(22) ú d à pp á : 'removing from fire'

(a)

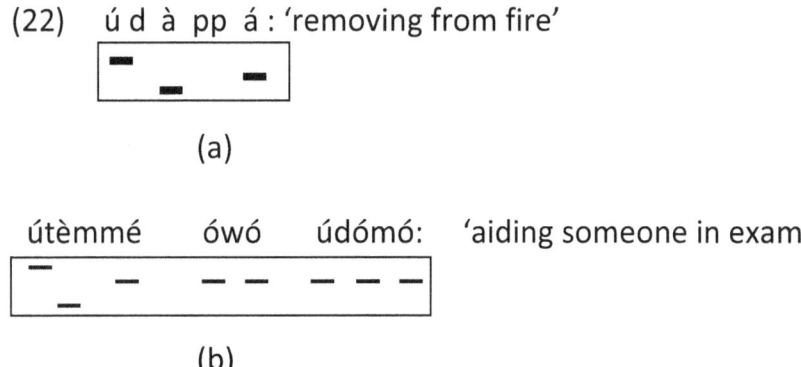

útèmmé   ówó   údómó: 'aiding someone in exam'

(b)

So in Ibibio, as indicated in (22a) above, the second high tone after the low tone on the second syllable of **údàppá** is downdrifted, i.e. there is a declination of this second high-tone on the third syllable compared with absolute high tone on the first high tone on /ú/. Downdrift is predictable, automatic and commonly regarded as intonational in the literature.

6.5.1.2.1.2 Downstep

This, however, indicates a situation in which a high tone has 'declined', or has been lowered in value yet there is, at least on the surface, no preceding low tone to mark the division from the preceding high tone, which is articulated at the normal 'absolute' value (according to Kenstowicz 1994). Consider the following Akan example taken from Dolphyne (1988:59)

(23) Kòfi 'dan: 'Kofi's house'

where the vertical stroke 'preceding the syllable that contains /a/ indicates a downstepped high tone.

Observe that a sequence of downstepped high tones looks like the steps in a stair-case, as the Ibibio example in (22b) shows.

While downdrift is commonly treated as predictable, as we have already said above, downstep is analysed as phonemic in many African languages, especially in West Africa. In Efik of the Efik-Ibibio-Annang Cluster, there is a minimal pair involving an absolute high tone and a downstepped high tone, as given below:

(24) a. ɔ́bɔ́ŋ: 'Mosquito'
     b. ɔ́'bɔ́ŋ:- 'Chief'

It has been suggested that a downstepped high tone can be explained in terms of a HLH pattern or melody in the underlying representation in which the low is lost or deleted historically after having lowered the second and following high tone. In the case of Ibibio, we have argued in Essien (2005), as stated earlier, that there are facts and arguments to justify a mid tone analysis rather than a downstepped analysis. The arguments continue.

6.5.1.3 Tone and intonation

Language is often erroneously divided into tone languages and intonation languages with tone operating as speech melody at the word level while intonation operates at the sentence or phrase level (cf. Abercrombie 1967). The coronally with some scholars is that tone languages have no intonation of the kind comparable to what is found in English between a statement/assertion and question such as the following.

(25)   a.   'This is the place!'
               'This is the place?'

However, some linguists have grudgingly conceded that some African tone languages with downdrift discussed in 6.1.2.1 above have intonation. But Essien (1989 1990) has argued that if we ignore the narrow interpretation of what constitutes intonation, many African languages do in fact have intonations besides the downdrift. Referring specifically to Ibibio, Essien (1990.60) has said this

> Even if Ibibio does not normally distinguish between declarative sentences i.e. sentences that make statements and interrogative ones (cf. Essien 1989),

it certainly does employ intonation for certain syntactic/semantic function, as other languages such as English do.

Essien (1989) vigorously and convincingly argues that Ibibio does make use of pitch and other devices, like Chinese and Thai but unlike European languages, to create interesting intonational patterns. The most common of this is what he refers to as the 'O' intonation pattern, the perception of which eluded Welmers (1973:41): he merely described it as" a sentence final particle... which suggests courtesy or personal interest" in Efik, a Niger-Congo language of the Efik-Ibibio-Annang cluster. Other Nigerian linguists (personal communication) have reported the existence of the phenomenon in their own languages confirming my suggestion of intrusion of it in a great many Nigerians' oral English such as the following:

(26)   a.   I didn't know it – o
               (in case you thought so)

       b.   He deceived me – o
               (He deceived me, you know)

The examples below show how this phenomenon occurs in Ibibio

(27)   a.   ḿmàákịt   ènyé-òò
            1stp past see him/her/it
            '1 saw him/her/it (you know)

       b.   Ówó ódò ikídiighe -oo
            Person the NegPref + come + Ng - oo
            'The man didn't come you known'

The influence on the English examples in (26) seems quite obvious from the African examples in (27), at least from the Ibibio perspective.

6.6 Morphology and syntax

Morphology has to do with word structure and syntax with sentence or phrase structure. But as Essien (2006) has argued, since syntax is derived from the Greek word *Syntaxis* meaning arrangement, there is syntax in phonology, morphology and syntax proper. As we shall soon see, morphology and syntax are so interwoven in most African languages, we have considered it economic to treat the two areas of core linguistics together.

Morphologically African languages are commonly known to have many inflectional and derivational markers in sentences unlike a lot of European languages. As a young undergraduate in Nigeria, I read a religious magazine known as 'The Plain Truth', published in the US, which examined the morphological complexities of African languages and concluded that the situation arose as a curse. We make no comment on that.

6.6.1 Language types

Dimmenaal (2000) has done quite modern and useful work on morphology (or morphosyntax) of African languages. Structurally, in particular paradigmatically, he identified Bantu languages, in particular Swahili, where the morphemes of words in sentences come one after another and can reasonably be segmented into morphemic units or morphs; Hausa, where such easy segmentation is not possible involving so called portmanteau morphemes); and thirdly what he refers to as extended exponence.

Let us now look at the morphology common in Bantu languages and some non-Bantu languages of the Niger-Congo family taking one example from Swahili, one of the largest and best known African languages spoken in east and southern Africa. It is a Niger-Congo language.

(28) ni- me – ji - funza   Ki – Swahili
ISG – ANT – REFL –learn CL 7 - Swahili
'I have learnt/taught myself Swahili'

As can be seen clearly there are clear discrete morphemes marking the first person singular (1SG) **n** I, the completion of action marker (so-called ANT) **me**, the reflexive (REFL) marker - **ji** and the root/stem **funza**. Also, nouns in Swahili usually take a noun marker and in our example in (28) above, that is **ki** contracting with 'Swahili person', M-Swahili (Sing), Wa - Swahili (Plural). The Ibibio example in (29) below is similar to the Swahili example.

(29) ḿm-dép   m-mótò
     ISG-Past-buy NPref-car
     'I bought a car'

where **m-** stands for the first person singular and PAST stands for the past tense and **m-** nominal prefix.

Perhaps we should point out that since the inflectional and derivational morphemes are bound morphemes, the examples in (28) and (29) in fact constitute one word each in Swahili and Ibibio, respectively.

Before we discuss portmanteau morphemes and extended exponence, we examine nominal classification, or noun class as evident in Ki-swahili .Nominal classification has to do with the fact that in many languages of Africa, particularly Niger-Congo languages, nouns have roots/stems and affixes by which these nouns can be divided into a number of classes which differ from each other in a variety of grammatical constructions. The nature and functions of these noun classes – and to some extent their form – show a number of striking similarities even when languages belonging to rather distantly related groups are compared. For Creissels (2000:242) nominal classification systems have nouns which are divided into several subsets on the basis of the fact that several types of noun modifiers have alternate forms to indicate agreement with the noun they modify. Simply, nominal classification is language specific categorization of nouns according to their formal grammatical properties commonly expressed by affixes.

According to Welmers (1973:159), in any Bantu languages; a very large number of noun forms can readily be analysed as consisting of a prefix and a stem. It may be possible to recognize from ten to twenty different prefixes in a given language. Many noun stems occur with two of these prefixes indicating singular and plural nouns. Some stems may, however, occur with only one prefix. These are usually mass or uncountable nouns, abstract nouns and other types for which counting seems irrelevant. In addition there are some stems with more than two prefixes. Such a variety reflects semantic differences in addition to number.

Consider the following examples of typical pairs of singular-plural nouns with their associated singular plural affixes (cf. Welmers 1973:161)

(30) a. m-ti: 'a tree'
     b. mi-:   'trees'

(31) a. ki-ti: 'a (wooden) stool'
     b. vi-ti: 'stools'

Occurrences of this type make it difficult to say that a particular stem belongs in a particular noun class. Rather, a given stem occurs, along with many other stems, in conjunction with a particular or pair of prefixes, and perhaps also with other prefixes or pairs of prefixes as well. The classification of nouns is not inherent in noun stems as such but is rather associated with prefixes.

Still according to Welmers (1973:161), in a Bantu language, most of the noun prefixes function as members of singular-plural pairs, though the pairing is evident only statistically, not on any formal basis. That is there is nothing that all singular prefixes or all plural prefixes have in common with each. For some pairs, there is at least a partial semantic correlation. In many Bantu language grammars, accordingly, it has been considered convenient to say that a pair of prefixes, singular and plural, represents one 'class' of nouns. In addition, there may be some "classes" with only one prefix, reflecting identity of singular and plural or the absence of numerical distinction. Following this type of statement, Swahili is generally said to have six nouns classes. In the following outline of these classes, /ɸ/ is an allomorph of a prefix which appears as /ji-/ before monosyllabic stems as /i-/before some vowel – initial stems, /N-/ represents a complex of morphophonemic alternations affecting the beginning of stems; and allomorphs occurring before vowel initial stems are indicated, though in most cases they differ from given forms here, generally by simple morphophonemic rules. The usual gross outline of the Swahili noun-class system, then, is like this.

			Singular	Plural	
(32)a.	m-,	wa-	: m-tu	wa-tu	'person'
b.	m-,	m-	: m-zigo	mi-zigo	'load'
c.	ɸ-,	ma-	: tofali	ma-tofali	'brick'
d.	ki-,	vi	: ki-tasa	vi-tasa	'lock'
e.	N-,	N-	: ndizi	ndizi	'banana'
f.	u-,	N-	: u-bao	mbao	'plank'

There is a lot of literature on Bantu noun classification and names like Meinhof (1932), Doke (1935), Cole (1955), Guthrie (1948) are often mentioned. Some African languages outside the regions where Bantu languages are spoken, especially Efik, Ibibio and Annang were often referred to as Semi-Bantu, because of some evidence similar to the example in (32) above. Consider (33) below.

		Singular		Plural	
(33)a.	Efik:	è-dídèm:	'king'	n-dídem:	'kings'
b.	Ibibio:	á-bìà :	'expert'	m-bia:	'experts'
c.	Annang:	á-chín:	'child'	ntò:	'children'

Evidence like this is often considered as vestiges of Bantu-type of nominal classification in these languages.

We now return to another type of languages, which have so called portmanteau morphemes, ie morphemes into which several meanings are collapsed. In Hausa, Chadic and Afroasiatic, words cannot be segmented into separate discrete morphs with each morph representing a particular morpheme or meaning as it is easily done in Swahili. While it is easy to provide 'interlinear glossing' by separating morphemes with hyphens, in the case of Swahili, this is not the case for a language like Hausa because in a language like this, single morphemes do not necessarily form the most 'useful' basis for morphological analysis. First, it is not always possible to determine the boundary or juncture between two morphemes. Secondly, whereas in the Swahili case, we can easily detect the so-called anterior marker -**me**-, it is not immediately obvious from the Hausa pattern below (34) what the shape of the so-called perfective marker is; is it -**aa**-, -**in**, or -**n**? Third, a particular morpheme may be an exponent of more than one meaning, an exponent being a marker expressing a property in a word,. Since the segmentation into discrete morphemes is rather difficult in Hausa, we have to find an alternative way of describing meanings, or sememes involved. The element **taa** is an exponent of *gender*, being feminine (contrasting with **yaa** 'he', for example), *number* (sing rather than plural), *person* (third, rather 1st or 2nd person), and *aspect* (i.e. perfective, i.e. a process that has been completed instead of being in the imperfective, it in the process). Since all these meanings overlap in one unit or form, a so-called portmanteau, we are dealing with a cumulative exponence. We can represent these pieces of information in a slightly different way as (34) below:

(34) Hausa, Chadic, Afroasiatic
  a. táá kòòyí Hausa
     3SG:F:PERT learn
     She has learnt Hausa

  b. yaa kooyi Hausa
     3SG: M:PERF learn Hausa
     He has learnt Hausa

Fused exponent arises when a marker can be shown to result from the fusion or (partly) phonological merger of two adjacent morphemes. This is commonly represented by way of dot between interlinear glossing. This occurs in Turkana, a Nilotic language, where the third person marker for the past tenses <u>a</u>- fuses with the high front vowel of one class of verbs.

39.a -nyám: 'She has eaten (solid things)
    3:PAST-eat (verb root - nyám)

    ɛmíj: (S)he has eaten (fluid things)'
    3: PAST. eat. (verb root- imíj)

It is not always easy to distinguish cumulative from fused exponences synchronically. Diachronically, such morphologically complex markers, for example, the commonly observed portmanteau markers combining gender, case, definiteness and number in Afroasiatic languages may be interpreted as a way of economizing on morphological distinctions. We shall encounter more morphological examples as we consider genetic classification later in this series of lectures. One aspect of the morphology of African languages is that both morphology and syntax are often so interwoven that many linguists often take a morphosyntactic approach in descriptions and analyses. This is useful in languages with concord systems in which there is agreement between the subject or object and the verb, as in Ibibio, Efik and Annang and between the noun and noun modifier as in Bantu languages. Languages with portmanteau morphemes like Hausa and fused exponence also show the extent to which morphology and syntax can be related in some languages.

6.6.2 Ideophones

Ideophones are probably the most intriguing category of words in African Languages, often defined as the first set of European Africanists perceived them as odd, unusual or irregular especially at the phonological level. Such words are found in most Niger-Congo languages, Nilo-Saharan languages as well as in Chadic languages (of the Afroasiatic phylum) though apparently not in Khoisan languages. According to Welmers (1973:461) ideophones prior to 1935, were given such labels as "interjections, "descriptive adverbs", "picture words", onomatopoeic adverbials" but the man who first suggested the term, Doke (1935) defined it or described it as "a vivid representation of an idea in sound, a word, often onomatopoeic, which describes a predicate, qualificative or adverb in respect to manner, colour, smell, action or intensity". Although Welmers is not very impressed with Doke's definition, we think in the light of more recent works on ideophones such as Ekere (1987) and Essien (1990), Doke has included some of the important features of this class of elements. For example, Essien (1990) has defined ideophones as:

> A class of words, often anomalous phonologically (as in the lengthening of final vowels or nasals) whose semantic function is the intensification of a situation, an apt, picturesque, epigrammatic or sense intensifying description. They may describe sounds, emotions, sights, smells, sensations or movements and they usually do this in the most economical and vivid way.

This is a characteristic of ideophones which Welmers (1974) has hardly mentioned in that monumental work of his. Since ideophones are not amenable to a precise and formal definition as admitted by nearly all scholars, the best we can do is to itemise some of the features of the elements.

(i) They are frequently phonologically anomalous. In some language, they may contain phonemes not found in the regular words of the language, or as Welmers (1973:462) puts it, "Unique sequences of phonemes and they may be aberrant in respect to rules of tone that apply to them." But as pointed out by Newman (1968:107), "it should be emphasized that the phonological distinctiveness of ideophones is a property of the set as a whole and not necessarily of each member of the set."

(ii) In many languages which have ideophones, these elements often behave grammatically like adverbs of manner like these beautiful ideophones in Ibibio.

(40)a. Éyo ákịm   kpək
'Light became darkness all of a sudden'

Ánám <u>nyám</u> ké ídém
'It came sensentionally to my body' = A certain sensation sized me.'

where **kpák** and **nyám** are quite normal phonologically, though as adverbs, they are not, because ordinary adverbs in the language are derived by reduplication from nouns or adjectives as **étó ètó**: 'stiffly' (derived from a full reduplication of **étó**: 'tree')

In Yoruba ideophones can serve as adjectives and nouns. There are some nominal ideophones in Ibibio.

(iii) Ideophones in many languages often have reduplicated forms as in the following example in the Igbo language, where kpam - kpam is ideophonic

(41) Ọ'gwu̱u̱la kpam-kpam:
'It's all'/ 'It is finished completely'.

This is quite common in Ibibio, Efik and Annang too.

(iv) Ideophones are often descriptive words " whose semantic functions is the intensification of a situation", as Essien (1990) has put it But that description is often apt, picturesque, epigrammatic, sense intensifying and supremely economical and sometimes vivid and electrifying.

(v) Some ideophones are onomatopoeic, i.e. imitations of actual sounds of objects or emotions of objects. For example, in Ibibio, the sound that a motor cycle makes when it is in motion is used to name it **kpǝk-kpǝk** (i.e. the object that makes that sound).

(vi) Related to onomatopia is what is described as phonaestheme, though according to Welmers (1973:462) this plays a rather minor role in ideophones in African languages. A phonaestheme is a sound or sequence of sounds recurring in a number of words in some way with the idea. For example, English /sn-/ is a phonaestheme associated with the nose in words like <u>sn</u>iff, <u>sn</u>iffle, <u>sn</u>uff, <u>sn</u>ore, <u>sn</u>icker. In the Ibibio language, the [dʒ] sound, which does not occur regularly in the language, except in emphatic stress and [kp] sound in some words with a low tone are usually associated with the sound of fall of a heavy object, as in (42) below.

(42) a.   Ọdùọ́   dʒ̀im
    'He/she/it fell dzim (i.e. heavily)

   b.   Ndikop kpùùb:
    'Suddenly I heard a heavy sound kpùùb'

(i) In some languages, like Yoruba, Defoid, Benue-Congo, Niger-Congo, ideophones appear only in unique collocations, and in general they seem to be semantically picturesque. For some types reduplication is optional and has an intensive function, sometimes suggesting some kind of irregularity, often but not always pejorative. These are all full reduplications of two-syllable sequences, as the following examples show:

(43) a. kpálakpala : 'nonsense'
    b. wokowoko : 'zig-zig'
    c. shákàshaka : 'shaggy'
    d. játijàt : 'worthless'

Observe the sameness of the repeated vowels as well as the unique tone sequence high-mid-low-mid in these examples, something similar to the tonal examples in Ibibio in (42) above. Observe the sound-sense or meaning relationship in these examples, a feature that reminds you that you are dealing with ideophones, words of a language in which the arbitrariess of the relationship between sounds and meaning is suspended in varying degrees.

Perhaps it is worth mentioning that while many ideophones can be translated into English or other European languages, some ideophones present quite serious translation problems, especially those that describe sounds, sensations, smells, sights or movements, as pointed out for Ibibio in Essien (1990:125).

6.7 Syntax

Notwithstanding what we have said at the end of 6.1 about the relationship between the morphology and syntax of African Languages, there is clearly a level of morphology and a level of syntax of African languages. The letter level, as we know, is concerned with how words and morphemes combine to form well-formed or grammatical sentences. Some of these words having more than one morpheme may be easily or conveniently segmentable or isolatable in sentences or phrases, as we have seen in the case of Swahili, probably the best known Bantu language spoken in East Africa; others not so easily done so, as we also saw in Hausa, a Chadic language widely spoken in Nigeria and many parts of West Africa, and Turkana, a Nilotic Nilo-Saharan language. This kind of state of affairs is not peculiar to African languages. Latin is often described as a fusional or inflecting language in terms of morphemic composition.

6.7.1 Basic sentence units in simple sentences

We use among other classes of words, nouns, verbs, adjectives, adverbs and prepositions or postpositions to form grammatical or well-formed sentences of a language. The other classes include pronouns, determiners, conjunction, intensifiers and interjections.

Words can modify other words and in the process serve as 'specifiers', 'complements' and 'modifiers' to form phrases or strings of words. The main word of the string serves as the head and in this way we have verb phrases and noun phrase, among others.

In African languages, nouns and verbs are the important lexical word classes. African languages tend to use verbs more frequently, more often than English, and Portuguese and other European languages do. For example, many descriptive adjectives in European languages are expressed by verbs in African languages or at least have a verbal form of the adjective. Thus in Aghem, a Grassfields Bantu, Benue-Congo, Niger-Congo language, (cf. Watters 2000:195) an English sentence like 'The bird is red' is not expressed as The bird BE red with the verb to be, but by a single verbal word, as the following example shows:

(44) nwin 'fi-báŋà nó   :   'The bird is red'
      bird CII-red: PRS: IC FOC

where CII stands for Class II, PRS, Present, IC, incomplete and FOC, Focus.

In Ibibio, however, there is no problem expressing it, as it is in English, except that the Ibibio equivalent would imply a contrastive emphasis as (45a) shows:

(45)   a. Ínúèn ódò ódò ìdàídàt
           Bird the 3PC-be red-red :
           'The Bird is red (rather than blue)'

where 3PC stands for third person concord (or agreement).

However, Ibibio has another way of rendering (45a), as (45b) below shows:

(45b) b. Ínúèn ódò ìdáídât :   'The bird is red'
         Bird the 3 PC-red-red

where ádáídât is the Verbal form of the adjective ádàídàt in (45a). Forms such as ìdáídât (derived from the root dàt) and 'fibáŋà in (44) are commonly referred to as verbal adjectives in African languages.

6.7.1.1 Basic word order in simple sentences

At some level, the term 'Subject' (S), 'Verb' (V) and 'object' (O) are used to described constituents of simple sentences. These are commonly considered from declarative, affirmative, active sentences with transitive verbs. Sentences with the basic word order do not have any words or phrases marked for emphasis or for any other special role.

According to Watters (2000:197), one study of the basic order in African languages (cf. Heine 1976) found out that of the 300 languages included in the study, 71% were SVO, 24% SOV, and 5% VSO.

The SVO order is common in Afro-Asiatic languages such as the Chadic languages (e.g. Hausa), in nearly all Niger-Congo subgroups (e.g. Swahili, Igbo, Yoruba, etc.)

except Mande, Senufo and Ijaw, and in a number of Nilo-Saharan languages such as Bari.

The second most common basic order in Africa is SOV. It is found in the Ethio-Semitic, Cushitic and Omotic languages within Afroasiatic, in the Senufo, Mande and Ijo languages of Niger-Congo as well as in Nilo-Saharan languages and in all the Khoe-subgroup of Khoisan. Consider this example from Sit'e, Ethio-Semitic, Afroasiatic.

(46) - - -S - - - - --- O ----   - - - V - - - -
      Išaan zɨt añe   gilgil Čeeňeet
      She: and nine   kids   she: gaive: birth
      'And she gave brith to nine kids'

The third basic word order, VSO, is uncommon. It is found primarily among the Berber. (in North Africa) and Chadic languages of Afroasiatic, the Nilotic, Surmic and Kuliak languages of Eastern Dusamic. Consider the example in (47) taken from Maasai, Eastern Nilotic, Eastern Sudanic, Nilo-Saharan.

(47) - V -   - - -S - - -   - -O - - -
      ɛdɔl   altí'ŋání   eŋkolii
      see   Person: Nom   gazelle : Acc
      'The person sees a gazelle' (cf. Watters 2000)

According to Watters, a common issue concerning basic word orders concerns the presence of the auxiliary (AUX) verb forms. Auxiliary verbs relate to the primary or main verb in sentence usually by indicating a tense or aspect or mood, but sometimes they have an adverbial function. Depending on how the given auxiliary verb behaves in the language, it may either serve as a 'specifier' in the VP, as in [AUX OV], or it might be the head of a larger ' auxiliary phrase' with the verb phrase as its complement, as in [AUX [O V]]. Whatever the structural details may be for a specific auxiliary verb, various languages with SVO as the basic order use the S-AUX-OV when an auxiliary is present.

Besides auxiliaries, word order involves the linear placement of additional objects (e.g. benefactives and locations) and adjuncts (e.g. prepositional or post positional phrases). In the case of languages that have two or more objects, languages with the more common SVO pattern usually place the additional object following the verb, giving a SVOO word order. Most often, the first object has a benefactive semantic role (i.e. the one who benefits from the situation) and is often referred to as the 'indirect object'.

As for locational and temporal phrases, sometimes they serve as the complements of a verb. An example would be: ' in the box' in the sentence 'He put the money in the box', where the verb 'put' requires a locational phrase. Many times, however, locational and temporal phrases are not complements but adjuncts of the sentence. In other words they provide optional clarification as to the place or time of the situation. Adjuncts of sentences in SVO languages generally follow the Object giving an SVOX word order, where 'X' represents one or more adjuncts. In some SOV languages, however, the adjunct precedes the verb, giving SXOV or SOXV order.

6.7.1.2 Cross-referencing NPs with VPs

Within sentences NPs and VPs may be related by some kind of cross-referencing. Most commonly this involves subjects and objects as NPs in relation to the verbs. This is why morphosyntactic descriptions and analysis, as we said earlier in section 5, are sometimes very useful.

In Benue-Congo languages, particularly the Bantu languages, Lower Cross languages, like Ibibio, Efik and Annang, and among Ethio-Semitic languages, a verb usually contains an affix that cross-references it to the subject noun phrase. This kind of obligatory cross-referencing is commonly referred to agreement or concord as we saw in the Ibibio example in (45a). The English 'He is' versus 'I am', morphosyntax is not very different from the phenomenon here: There is subject and verb agreement. In other languages of throughout Africa, however, agreement between the subject NP and VP is not present. Such languages include Niger-Congo languages in the sub-groups such as Mande, Adama Ubangi, Kru, Kwa, Gur and some Benue Congo subgroups like Mambiloid languages, as well as many Chadic languages and various Nilo-Saharan languages. These languages generally require an independent pronoun as an explicit subject when a subject noun phrase is present. (cf. Watters 2000:200). In those languages that observe agreement or concord, the subject NP can be deleted because its presence is guaranteed in the concord or agreement marker on the verb. Therefore in Ibibio, for example, the independent pronoun **ami** 'I' is deletable, as the brackets enclosing it indicate

(48) (Àmì) m-màá-kɨt   enye
       I   IPC-Past-see him/her/it
       I saw him/her/it'

where IPC stands for 1st person concord marker.

6.7.1.3 Commands & Questions

The basic order of sentences in 6.7.1.1 is for declarative sentences, as was pointed out there. But there are also other types of sentences in African languages as there are in the European languages. Such sentences that express command are in the imperative mood and those that ask questions are in the interrogative mood.

As for commands, the relevant points for syntax are that the subject of the sentence is usually deleted at the surface level but the verb often carries the number of the verb as shown in Ibibio below:

(49) a. dí :   'come' (singular)
   b. ì-dí : 'come' (Plural)

Interestingly, in that language, a very small number of nouns, including some personal names, can occur with the imperative form along with the verb, as in the following examples.

(50) a. Yi̯n, dàkká dá
   'Child, stand up'

 b. -Kôn, kéré ídém mfò
   Kon, worry self your
   'Kon, worry about yourself'

where the vowel prefixes (a-/ and /o-/ have been deleted from <u>áyin</u> and <u>Òkôn</u>, respectively.
   Watters (2000:203-2004) explicitly states that languages such as Silte', an Ethio-Semitic Afroasiatic language, Hausa and many West African languages from Mande, Gur and Kwa groups use different intonation patterns for yes-no question. It is surprising that Clements (2000), which is a work on the phonology of African languages, has no section on intonation and has only downdrift, or suspension of it, final lowering, boundary tones in a one line summary as manifestations of intonation and makes no reference to Essien (1989) on intonation in Ibibio. This information by Watters tacitly

supports my dissatisfaction with orthodox treatment of intonation in African languages by European and American Linguists.

6.7.2 Negation

This syntactic process operates on positive sentences, declarative, imperative or interrogative. But let us consider simple positive declarative ones. Since Klima (1964) identified two kinds of negation in English: sentence and constituent negation, this has been applied to other languages.

One common way of negating a sentence is to modify the verbal category by the use of an affix changing it from a positive to a negative verb. This kind of negation is found throughout the Benue-Congo languages. Consider, for example, (51) below taken from Watters (2000:206).

(51) Aghem, Grassfields Bantu, Benue-Congo, Niger-Congo.
    a.   óbó f-ghâm : ' He has hit the mat'
           3SGhit C7 –Mat

    b.   Oka bo ghâm-fɔ: ' He has not hit the mat'
           3SG NEG hit mat-C-7
           (demphesised noun form required with negatives)

In Ibibio, negation affects the form of the concord prefix on the verb, except the first person, as the following examples show (cf. Essien 1990).

(52) a. Òkôn â - kâ: Okon has gone
Okon 3PC – go

b. Okon i-kaa-ha : 'Okon has not gone
Okon NEGPREF-go-NEG SUF

In some languages, the verb may be doubly marked for negation, as in the following examples taken from Watters (ibid)] and Ibibio in (52a) above.

(53). Lobala, Bantu C, Benue-Congo, Niger-Congo
a. ba-tub-aka: 'They sang'
3PL-Sing-PST

b. te-ba-ik-aka tuba: 'They did not sing'
NEG-3 PL-NEG: AUX-PST Sing

These are instances described by Watters as negation internal to the verbal word. Negation external to the verbal word is found in Igbo, a Benue-Congo language, again supplied by Watters (2000:207).

(54) a. Ọ nà èri ň'ri : 'She is eating'
he/she IC eat food

b. Ọ nà-'ghe   èri   ň'ri: 'She is not eating'
    he/she IC-NEG eat food

where the negative suffix **-ghi** is attached to the incompletive particle **nà**.

6.7.1.5 Serial Construction
Since we are going to discuss serial construction in typological classification later, we shall not discuss it here to avoid a repetition.

6.7.1.6 Relative Clauses
Relative clauses are simple clauses which are embedded in a complex clause with a main or matrix clause. Such an embedded clause serves an adjectival function modifying the head noun, just as adjectives in an NP modify the head of the phrase.

Relative clauses may be restrictive or non-restrictive, such as 'the book that I wrote' and "the English book, which almost got lost". The distinction between restrictive and non-restrictive relative clauses is generally not marked in African languages. Non-restrictive clauses are preferably expressed by some kind of co-ordinate sentences or through some kind of apposition.

African languages display a range of ways to form relative clauses. Consider the following examples taken from Watters (2000:226).

(55) Swahili
S._ _ _ _ _ _ _ _ _ _ _   V ..... Pred Nom
   [... S..   -V - - - - -   --O - - - -]
Watu [amba –o   wa-li-m-piga Ahmed] ni washenzi
People [REL- C2 they - PST- him - hit Ahmed] are savages
'The people who hit Ahmed are savages'

(56) *Afar*   - - S - -
     [- S - - - - O - - - V ---   ]
     'Usuk / a'tu bah – 't –e   du' ye 'be – e
     he   you bring – you –PFV things took- he: PFV
'He took the things which you brought.'

In the Swahili example (55), the structure of the noun plus a relative clause is similar to that of English. The head noun (bolded) comes first, followed by the relative clause, indicated by the square brackets [. . .] The clause begins with a relative pronoun ambao. In languages with a basic SVO word order, the relative clause typically follows the head noun, as in Swahili.

In the Afar example (56), the order of the head noun and the relative clause is reversed with the clause preceding the head noun. This order is common in SOV languages. The head noun ' things' is the direct object of the main Verb and also the direct object in the relative clause. In both (55) and (56), where the head noun is realized outside... the relative clause, its matching noun phrase in the relative clause is absent, even in the form of pronoun whether the clause follows or precedes the head noun. This lack of a pronoun in the relative clause to cross - reference with the head noun of the relative clause is common when the head noun correlates with the subject or object of the relative clause.

There are other strategies for relativization and some languages may have more than one form of relative clause.

6.8 Pronominal System

Because of time constraint, we shall limit the discussion to the pronominal system in the Niger-Congo phylum, though some mention will be made of it in the genetic classification of the other three phyla-Nilo-Saharan, Afroasitic and Khoisan later.

Some pronouns are referred to as independent or free pronouns, while others are referred to as dependent pronouns, which are attached to verb forms as subject or object makers by which the subject or object can be identified, though not present in the sentence. As we have shown earlier such dependent pronouns are in fact agreement or concord markers in a morphosynatic analysis. An examination of the linguistic features of the Niger-Congo languages shows the following pronoun systems the families, branches, groups, etc that constitute the Niger-Congo phylum.

(a) *Ijoid*. There are traces of inalienable/alienable relationship, i.e. relationship existing between a possessor and the object possessed which is intimate (and therefore inalienable) e.g. between an individual and his/her parts of the body, or between a person and his/her relatives. The relationship between a person and the objects he/she possess is alienable (i.e. can be 'dispensed with'). In these languages new gender system, always distinguish feminine human from masculine, sometimes masculine from neuter, or in singular, reflected in determiners. When we are talking about alienable versus inalienable relationship, we are concerned with the possessive pronouns in these languages.

(b) *Dogon*. The languages have one basic set, with object, possessive and embedded sets derived.

(c) *Kru*. Human/ non-human distinction common in the pronominal system.

(d) *Gur*. Sometimes the pronouns are inclusive/ exclusive, and 2nd singular often #ino (as in Kru, Senifo, Kasen (Gur) contrasting normal 1st singular #mi.

(e) *Kwa*. Independent, subject, object, possessive. Animate / non-animate common in the 3rd person.

(f) *Benue-Congo*. These languages have independent, subjects, objects and possessive pronouns. In embedded clauses, there are relative and logophoric or self-referring pronouns as in the following examples in Efik and Ibibio.

(57)a. Owo emi nyomde odu ke Abuja
Person Rel. Pro Ist per want+Rel. marker is in Abuja
'The person that I'm looking for is in Abuja.'

b. Ete obo ke imọ ikikood enye
Father 3rd per said that log pro C + call him
'Father 3rd per said that he (father) called him'

where **emi** is a relative pronoun and **imọ** a logophoric or self-referring pronoun in Efik and Ibibio, respectively. The logophoric pronouns **imọ** (pl mmimo) disallows ambiguity of the kind one finds in the English sentence below:

(58) John said that he would go

where <u>he</u> in the complement sentence can refer to John or someone else. The non-logophoric form of imọ/mmimọ is enye/ọmmọ (he/they) or afo/ndufo (you/you) in Ibibio.

g. *Cross River*. These languages have independent, subject, object and possessive pronouns.

h. *Bantoid*. 3rd person concord with noun classes are the pronominal elements in these languages, perhaps we should consider one or two examples of inventories of pronoun systems in two Benue-Congo languages, namely Igbo and Ibibio.

Igbo
(59) a. mmụ : `I'   anyi: 'we'
     b. gị : `you (sg)      ánù : `you' (Pl)
     c. ya : `he, she, it'  ha :  `they'

These forms are also used as possessives, as the following examples show:

    éwú ya : `his goat'    úlò yá : ` his house

As verbal objects, the same forms (in 59) are used except for the first person singular, which is a syllabic /m/, as in the following example:

(61) ọkpọọ m' : `he called me'

As verbal subjects, the plural forms listed above (in 59) are again used. The second person form is /i/ or /ị/, depending on vowel harmony. The third person form is /O/ or /ọ/. In some constructions, the first person is /m/. In other constructions, the first person form consists of /a/ or /e/ before the verb plus a syllabic /m/ after the verb. Consider the following examples:

(62) a. I méé iya   'if you do it'
     b. Ọ bụ ìtè   'It is a pot'
     c. M mee iya   'if I do it'
     d. E méélá m ya   'I have done it'
     e. A hụrụ m ya   'I saw him'

Perhaps to be identified with the vowel component of the first person form above is an impersonal subject pronoun, /a/ or /e/.

Let us now consider the inventory of the Ibibio personal pronoun system, which is somewhat similar to the Igbo.

Ibibio

(63) a. Àmì: 'I'   mnyin: 'we'
     b. Àfò: 'you' (sg)   ndùfò : 'you' (Pl)
     c. ènyé: 'he/she/it'   Ommọ : 'they'

The plural forms are also used as possessives but in the singular the forms undergo some changes as possessive adjectives, as the following examples show:

(64) a. mmotò mnì
          car my   =   "my car"

      b. útóm mfò
          work your   =   "your work"

      c. Èkà ọmò
          mother his/her   =   'his/her mother'

Observe the order of words N + possessive adjective.

As verbal objects, the singular forms also undergo some changes in form, as the following examples show but the plural subjects and objects remain the same. Consider the following examples:

65.a. nsák mîìn/mìèn   ìsák ńnyìn
       laugh at me   laugh at us

  b. úsàk fụ̀ìn/fìèn
      he/she is laughing at you (sg)
      ísàk ndufo
      'he/she is laughing at you'

  c. ásâk ènyé
      he/she is laughing at you
      ásâk ọmmọ
      he/she is laughing at them

6.9 Some parts of speech system
6.9.1 Adjectives

As we already indicated above, in many African languages, nouns and verbs are the important lexical word classes. But adjectives do occur frequently all the same. As noted in that section many descriptive adjectives in European languages are commonly expressed by verbs in many African languages. Some languages (like Ibibio and Efik) have two forms for descriptive adjectives; the adjective proper form and the verbal form agrees with the noun it modifies in number and person, as most verbs do. These are commonly referred to as verbal adjectives.

As Creissels (2000:249) has observed:

> As regards adjectives as a category, a striking peculiarity of African languages (particularly the Niger-Congo phylum) is that they have a very small number of non-derived adjectives…. And no possibility of deriving adjectives from other categories at all. For example, Igbo has eight adjectives, semantically, four pairs of antonyms: úkwú 'large'/ ńtà 'small' … ọma 'good' ọjọọ 'bad' and ọcà 'light-coloured'/oji 'dark colour'.

It is also not uncommon in African languages to see adjectives very morphologically similar to nouns. For example, in Bantu languages, the gender-number prefixes attached to adjectives are identical to those attached to nouns, since in these languages nouns and adjectives show agreement between them through their prefixes. By contrast, the other types of modifiers have distinct gender-number prefixes, at least in some cases.

Because of the tendency of many African languages to have limited inventories of adjectival lexemes, many notions expressed by adjectives in many languages of the world tend to be encoded through adjectives. Wolof, spoken in Senegal, which virtually has no category of adjectives, is one example. On the other hand, Ibibio adjectives, as we have already shown above can be expressed in both adjectival and verbal forms. Where it is expressed adjectivally, it usually agrees with the noun in number, as it does in Bantu languages. In Ibibio, some of the adjectives can only be expressed in reduplicated forms, as the following examples.

66.   ì dàĭdàd: 'red'
      onio-onio: 'yellow'

Such adjectives are usually colour adjectives.

6.9.2 Adverbs

Most African languages have a rather limited number of one-word adverbial referring to time and place and fewer still referring to manners, means or categories. Note the following

1. Nearly all African languages have temporal expressions for *now, yesterday* and *tomorrow*, though in quite a number of languages yesterday and tomorrow may be ambiguous.

In a language like Kpelle, a Mande language spoken in Liberia, /wέɛ/: 'yesterday', /sâa/: 'today', and /tínà/: 'tomorrow', these temporal adverbs share certain special characteristics and are comparable to temporal expressions in many African languages.

On the other hand, according to Welmers (1973:447), some languages have single words or expressions for such time reference as 'day before yesterday', 'day after tomorrow' and even farther removed from today. Swahili has the forms /jana/ 'yesterday', /leo/ 'today', /kesho/ 'tomorrow' then a phrase /kesho kutwa/ 'day after tomorrow' but /mtondo/ 'three days from today, while Ibibio has /ákịd/' for 'several days ago'. Outside Niger-Congo, Hausa can cover an entire week with six single words and only a phrase as given below (cf. Welmers 1973:447-8).

67. a. shékáràn jiya: 'day before yesterday; then'
    b. jíyà 'yesterday'
    c. gòbé: 'tomorrow'
    d. jíbí: 'two days from today'
    e. gátà: 'three days from today'

f. citta: 'four days from today'

Nearly all African language also have locative adverbs such as the following in Kpelle:

68. ɓɛ: 'here' (b) nāa: 'there' and (c) māna: 'over there; Ibibio also has similar three locative adverbs, as in the following examples:

69a. mí: 'here' (b) dó: 'there'
(c) kó: 'yonder (away from speaker, and hearer)'

Interestingly, this language (cf. Essien 1990) grammaticalizes location as the following examples show:

70. a. Dídítêm ùdiá
 come-lock + cook
 'come here and cook food'

 b. Fèghé kékít ènyé
 run loc + see him
 'Run there to see him'

Virtually, no mention is made of adverbs of manner beyond ideophones in African language in the literature. And yet Ibibio, Efik, Annang and quite a number of Lower Cross languages do have adverbs commonly created by reduplication of nouns, as the following examples in Ibibio show:

71.a. *Nouns*   *Adverbs*
      étó: 'tree'   étó-ótó: 'stiffly (like a tree)'

    b. ínèm: 'sweatness'   ínèm-inèm: 'sweetly'
      àfái: 'wildness'   àfáai-àfái: wildly

As we have already, pointed out in 6.2, some ideophones behave like adverbs grammatically, as this example in Ibibio demonstrates.

72.   Ásʌk   ásáńà   nìọk-nìọk   ádî
      3P+still 3p+walk slowly and heavily 3P+come
      'He was still walking slowly and heavily coming'

6.10 Verbal system

We have come across some aspects of the verbal in the foregoing sections of this chapter. We now examine it in some more details. As we have already observed, African languages tend to use verbs frequently, certainly more frequently than European languages do. Thus as already observed, many descriptive adjectives in European language are expressed in verbal forms in some African languages and both in verbal and adjectival forms in others. In addition, what are expressed in preposition, conjunction, comparative, etc. forms take verbal forms in many African languages.

In most African languages, the verb has more complex conjugations than any other category. The verb may have rich inflection even in languages which nominal inflection proper does not exist. African languages which are devoid of inflections are therefore rare.

There are, however, a few African languages that have no verbal inflection. One such language is Zarma, a Nilo-Saharan language (cf. Creissels 2000:238).

73. fà:ti si   fojOhin à 'Faati won't cook the soup'
    faati IMPERF NEG: Soup. DEF Cook

In this language, tense, aspect, modality and negation makers cannot be analyzed on verb affixes.

6.10.1 Inflection and types

According to Creissels (2000:238), the proportion of languages with predominantly or even exclusively prefixal inflection is higher in Africa than in most parts of the world. In addition, verbal inflections in African languages also have tonal alternations. Thus, in Kposo, a Kwa, Niger-Congo language, the distinction between a positive and a negative sentence may rely exclusively on tonal variations of the subject marker prefixed to the verb, as the example in (74) shows:

74. ū-dzí   'we have eaten'
     ūū-dzi 'we have not eaten'

As regards types of verbal inflections, three have been distinguished:

i.   A vast majority of African language have subject and object as well as other affixes.

ii. There are some languages, like the Mande languages, with verbal inflections involving no subject or object.

iii. Systems of verbal inflection consisting exclusively of subject and object markers are extremely rare both at the world level and among African languages.

Tense, aspect, modality (abbreviated as TAM by Creissels 2000) are commonly marked or lexicalized in African language as verbal inflection. In many of these languages like Igbo, Hausa, Swahili, etc aspect and tense are commonly so intertwined that they are generally treated as tense/aspect. But in Ibibio tense and aspect are separable, for the most part, because they are separate markers for tense and aspect. In the cases where tense and aspect are interwoven and expressed in one form, it may be possible to see aspect or tense as primary and the other as secondary or what Comrie (1985) refers to as implicature. The same analysis can be made of a marker that combines temporal (i.e. tense) and modal meanings.

A number of scholars see a relation between tense/aspect and focus, i.e. special emphasis on a sentence constituent (cf. Watters 2000:214) resulting in the use of one set of tense markers or alternants, or another. Where a sentence has a particular focus, a particular verbal form is used, and where it doesn't another particular verbal form is used, according to Watters. Focus is of course a discourse or pragmatic matter concerned with the most importance or salient information in the sentence. In our opinion, this cannot be the only factor responsible for the alternation of tense/aspect marking, especially in a language like Ibibio, as we shall see presently. For the benefits of a wider perspective on tense or tense/aspect in African languages, let us consider Essien (2006) in which he posed this question as a section of his paper.

6.10.2 Auxiliary focus or syntactic conditioning of tense allomorphs?

In English and other European languages, we are used to looking at tense with its morphological realizations in terms of allomorphs which are either phonologically or morphologically conditioned. In many African languages, however, there is what is referred to as a curious interplay between tense (or tense/aspect) and focus (cf. Hyman and Watters 1984:233) on the one hand, and what is regarded as syntactic intervention in phonology by Essien and Zima in a series of their publications. Hyman and Watters go on to say this, "while the exact realization of this interplay varies from language to language, in each case some parameter of focus determines which of the two corresponding sets of these tense-aspect markers is used in a given situation. In this way, the feature [+ focus} can be used to characterized some constructions."

On the other hand, Essien and Zima in a series of publications (cf. Essien 1983, 1990a, 1990b, 1991a, 1991b, 1995 etc and Zima 1967, 1971, 1986, 1995) individually and independently see some higher level of conditioning of allomorphs or alternants of tense/aspect morphemes. Perhaps I should mention that Hyman and Watters (1984) make no mention whatsoever of either Essien 1983 or Zima 1967 and 1971, which were published before their work in 1984.

Let us begin with the summary of Essien's position. According to him, the Ibibio tense system is characterised as follows:

a. It is a three-way opposition of past, present, and future.

b. the past is represented by the allomorph or variant -màá- or -ké, the occurrence of which is determined by the absence or presence of categories such as negation, wh-question, mood, inceptive or progressive aspect, and some form of emphasis, or focus. Essien finds it inconceiveable how these various categories which have their own different semantic interpretations can be conflated by or subsumed under one category of focus in Ibibio, as predicted by the Hyman-Watters analysis.

c. The future tense is represented by -yàá/yáá- or dîi-, the occurrence of which is conditioned by the absence or presence of the same set of categories – negation, wh-question, mood, inceptive and progressive aspects, and some form of emphasis (or focus in Hyman and Watter's terminology).

d. The present tense is represented by me- or ɸ (zero) allomorph. Interestingly, the same set of environments that determine the occurrence of -màá- and -yàá/yáá- and of -ke-, -dîi- also determine the occurrence of the ɸ (zero) allomorph of the present tense. In the present tense, therefore, the alternation in between the presence and the absence of an overt morphological marker.

e. There is a distributional equivalence of the allomorphs of the sort below:
-me-: ɸ what -màá- ke- and what-yàá-/yáá-: dîi

Zima (1967), on his own part, has given one of the clearest examples of the alternation of verbal forms, conditioned, in our view, by the syntax of the Hausa language, a Chadic language, unlike Ibibio, which is a Benue-Congo language. According to him:

> The most clear example case of syntactic alternation is obviously represented by **sunàà** and **sukèè** forms. As discovered by many authors, those two forms are used in Hausa in complementary distribution. The **sukèè** form occurs in a sum of environments which may be defined as follows: (a) the relative constructions… (b) The so-called emphatic constructions… (c) Questions introduced by interrogative word particles…

These Hausa examples of syntactic conditioning of tense aspect allomorphs show that this phenomenon is not limited to Niger-Congo languages, as Creissels seems to suggest. Comrie (1985:7), unaware of Zima's works and mine, alludes to the existence of this phenomenon in Bantu languages in this way:

> In the grammar of some languages, moreover, the term tense has a wider range of use. For example many Bantu languages are described as having special tenses for use in relative clauses and special negative tense.

In the light of what we now know of the tendency in some languages for allomorphs of tenses (or tenses/aspects) to alternate in accordance with the presence or absence of some categories like negation, Comrie's comment must be taken as a reflection of the syntactic conditioning of allomorphs of tense/aspect morphemes in negative, relative and many other constructions as highlighted above. When, therefore Hyman and Watters (1984:236)) say that "it can be safely assumed that languages can have two sets of corresponding tense-aspect markers, one set occurring under focus, the other not under focus", they are tacitly admitting syntactic conditioning of these tense-aspect markers.

What seem clear whether from the auxiliary focus analysis, or the syntactic conditioning analysis is that in many African language, there are parallel tense/aspect markers which occur under certain mutually exclusive syntactic environments. In either analysis, these environments have been clearly identified and they are identical.

The major difference seems to be in the approach: Hyman and Watters (1984) seem to approach it from a semantic view point. For example, they talk of "the interaction between focus and semantic features of tense, aspect, mood and polarity", while Essien and Zima clearly do so from the point of view of the interplay between syntax and phonology, a relationship linguists working on African languages cannot afford to ignore.

6.10.3 Verbal Extensions

Verbal extension is a morphological process which is common among Niger-Congo languages, particularly among Bentu languages. According to Ashton (1944:216), Swahili is a classic example of a Bantu language which has verbal extensions, as this quotation from her shows:

> The Swahili verb root is capable of rich... and varied development in the form of additional verb stem – each with its complement of conjugations, moods, tense, etc.

These extensions are usually suffixes. There are also cases of the existence of "a nucleus (or what Guthrie 1967:11)" calls 'core' or 'radical) as this except shows;

> A set of invariable cores or radicals, from which all the words are formed by agglutinating process, these radicals having the following features:
>
> a) They are composed of consonant vowel consonant
> b) When a grammatical suffix is attached to the radical, there is formed a 'base' on which words identifiable as verbals are built.

The 'nucleus' or 'radical' is either CVC or CV in a language like Ibibio, a Niger-Congo language, which has quite a number of verbal extensions or what Essien (1983) chooses to call derivatives, such as reflexive, reciprocal, causative, reversive, relative, etc. and these are also common verbal extensions of Bantu languages. Other non-Bantu languages in the Niger-Congo languages like Igbo also have them.

Below are some examples of how nouns and verbal extensions are derived from radicals or nuclei in Ibibio, a non-Bantu language.

75. Radical/nucleus   Derived Noun   Derived verb
    a. *dap   ń-dáp: 'a dream'   dáp-pá 'dream'
    b. *dịk   n-dịk: 'a fear'   dịk-ké: 'frighten'
    c. *yai   ù-yài: 'beauty'   yài-yá: 'be beautiful'

According to Williamson and Blench (2000:10), verbs in Niger-Congo languages commonly end in suffixes (like verbal extensions) that modify their meaning and often vallency.

6.10.4 Argument structure of verbs

Every predicate has its argument structure. That is every lexical or main verb is specified for the number of arguments it requires. The arguments are the participants minimally involved in the activity or state expressed by the predicate or the verb. The notion of 'participants in an activity' has been formalized on the basis of the approach commonly adopted in formal logic. The arguments of a predicate are realized by noun phrases (NPs). The arguments structure of verbs or predicates replaces the notions of transitivity, distransitivity, and intransitivity.

In regard to transitivity-intransitivity, many verbs in African languages would normally be transitive whereas in English and I suspect in other European languages, like Portuguese – they would be intransitive. Verbs such as go, sleep, run, come, laugh, etc., are always transitive in most African language and therefore are two-place predicates. They, at least, attract a cognate object and are translatable as the following 'go a place' 'sleep a sleep', 'laugh a laugh', etc.

An argument position is structurally accessible to theta-role assignment, according to Chomsky 1986. So argument positions are NP positions and theta positions as well. But not all NP positions are accessible to theta-role assignment, because theta roles, according to Sells (1985) "are written into lexical entries of heads [in the lexicon] and are known as argument structures".

Two types of arguments are found in the literature. These are internal and external arguments. The internal argument as object of the verb represented as [V, NP] while the external argument is the NP argument which is outside the VP, i.e. the subject. Very little is available of argument structure of verbs on African languages. But the concord between subjects and verbs and verbs and objects especially in many Niger-Congo languages, as we have seen above and will see later on geneti classification, are interesting for the modern generative grammarians.

6.10.5 Stative non-stative verbs

According to Essien (1990:65), stativity and nonstativity are both aspectual features commonly ascribed to verbs. While stativity is inherently durational, nonstativity is not. Stativity describes a state or a static non-changing situation for a period. Stativity therefore implies duration. On the other hand, non-stativity expresses the non-static character of verbs or predicates. Non-stative verbs are, therefore, active, 'doing' verbs expressing activity (cf. Huddleston 1976:241) and describing what has come to be known as dynamic situations (cf. Comrie 1976:48 and Lyons (1977:706ff).

Expatiating on static situations expressed by stativity and dynamic situations expressed by nonstativity, Comrie says that the phases of a state are typically identical involving little or no change, whereas the phases of a dynamic situation are different, characteristically changing and above all, in his own words, "requiring a continual input of energy if they are not to come to an end" (p.13).

African languages have ways of making the stative - nonstative distribution in their structures and here are two which have been studied in this connection. Consider what Welmers (1973:257) said about Yoruba.

Beyond this point, however, it is necessary to distinguish between transitive and intransitive verbs – or perhaps between verbs indicating action and verbs indicating state. For each type, it is possible to use the reduplicated form of a verb after a noun, but the underlying structure of the resultant phrases is quite different. With a transitive, the phrase indicates the action designated by the verb and the noun is the object of the action. With an intransitive verb indicating state, the phrase has the structure of a noun and an attributive, as in the following examples:

   išu jije: 'the eating of yams'
   igi giga: 'a tall tree'

Verbs indicating a state differ in other respects from verbs indicating action. In the simple construction of a subject pronoun and a verb stem, a verb indicating action refers to past time but a verb indicating sate refers to present time.

So it does appear a difference in reduplication and alternation between past time and present time in Yoruba differentiate between nonstative and stative verbs.

 Igbo also makes a distinction between what Igbo linguists refer to as active verbal radicals and stative radicals. For them active verbal radicals express actions like -ri: 'eat', -gwa: 'tell', -zà 'sweep', -hu: 'see', -me: 'do', and stative verbal radicals express states, qualities and existential notion of being e.g. -da: 'fall', -fu: 'be lost', -nwe: 'have', -no: 'stay', bu: 'be'.

In Ibibio, stative verbs include verbal adjectives (cf. 6.9.1) such as yàiyá: 'be pretty' and nyɔ́ɔ́n: 'be tall' and a sub-class of verbs referred to as 'verbs of inert perception' by Comrie (1976:35) such as diọọñọ: 'know', kòp: 'hear' and kit: 'see'.

In conclusion on morphosyntax, we would like to say that much of the interaction between morphology and syntax arises from the important roles of nouns, verbs and adjectives, which quite often behave like verbs. In most languages in Africa there is what Creissels (2000:235) calls subject/object indexation typology by which affixes are attached to verb forms. But as we have said in 6.10.2, there could also be an interface between phonology and syntax.

6.11 Classification of African languages

Before Greenberg published his *The Languages of Africa*, in 1963, described by Welmers (1973:1) as "the most important, the most comprehensive and the most widely accepted genetic classifications of languages in Africa," others had shown interest in African languages. We return to Greenberg later below.

Before Greenberg's, authoritative work, the classification of African languages had been unduly concerned with the hypothesis of language mixture, that is that the languages available at the time of description to the scholars came about as a result of some mixture of some languages x and y (or perhaps more) resulting in the present state of language z. We will consider some examples. According to Welmers (1973), perhaps the most dramatic and ridiculous of examples of linguistic speculation is provided by Sir Harry Jonston (1919:29) who is quoted as having said this: "A great jumble of events, and lo!– new languages spring into existence" He noted that languages scattered all over West Africa have systems of noun classes with varying degrees of concord somewhat similar to the well-known concord system of Bantu languages. For Sir Harry Johnston, then, the best developed and most regular Bantu languages represented the oldest and most original proto-Bantu type. In his speculation, he said that a very long time ago, speakers of this proto-Bantu Language had some contact with West African peoples and their languages, which were unrelated to Bantu. However, in his opinion these original West African Languages unrelated to Bantu, overnight acquired what Welmers describes as "entire chunks of Bantu morphological structure and a small amount of their most basic vocabulary" by fusion. Within West Africa itself, Johnston also speculated that the More language, an Upper Volta language, which has a suffix-marked class system, was once unrelated to Fula (or Fulfulde) but strangely borrowed the entire noun class system – as a morphological structure and concept! – from Fula.

Johnston apparently believed that theoretically society can consciously change its language substantially structurally.

Malcom Guthrie (1962) came up with a similar theory of language mixture. For Guthrie (1962), according to Welmers (1973:2), the obvious grammatical and lexical similarities between the West African languages in question and Bantu languages are due to what he, Guthrie, described as "the incorporation of Bantu features into languages of a distinct origin" in the form of "grammatical contamination and "loan words". When we come to Greenberg's classification, it will be obvious that Guthrie was simply speculative.

Carl Meinhof (1940:164), much in the tradition of the mixed language hypothesis, went as far as to suggest that "Bantu is a mixed language… Descended of a Hamitic father and a Negro mother.", a suggestion based culturally rather than linguistically. In addition, the so-called Nilo-Hamitic and so-called Semi-Bantu languages of West Africa are more or less ingrained in the mixed languages theory of Africa. In what seems obviously strange to us today, E.O.J. Westphal (1957) claimed that "a given language may be most closely related to one language phonologically, to another morphologically, and still another lexically." For Westphal, genetic relationships of the kind postulated by Greenberg (as we shall see later) was inconceivable while

M.A. Bryan (1959) has merely used these theories as the basis for positing extensive language mixtures in Africa and thereby rejecting the basis for Greenberg's genetic classification in the process.

Even in 1966, three years after the publication of Greenberg's work. David Dalby still rejected the traditional concept of genetic relationship and genetic classification. Rather he argued that as genes in human hereditary have a multiple origin, so one should not be surprised to discover multiple origins in existing languages reinforcing the arguments for language mixtures. He cited pidgin and creole languages (like Krio of Sierra Leone) and the unusual case of Mbugu in East Africa as unquestionable instances of mixed languages. Perhaps I should point out here that Greenberg and those who accepted his theory and worked within it did not use 'genetic' in association with 'genes or 'genealogy' in the way Dalby did but rather associated it with 'genes' or origin and 'genetic relationships' have to do with linguistic characteristics that are inherited by one generation of speakers from another, vis-à-vis those which are acquired from other sources.

6.11.1 Greenberg's classification of African languages

From available evidence, Greenberg had been involved in the classification of African Languages since 1955 when he published a book entitled *Studies in African Linguistic Classification*. In 1963, he published his *The Languages of Africa*, his best known publication on African Linguistics.

Welmers (1973:1) describes it as "the most important, most comprehensive and most widely accepted classification of the languages of Africa." Earlier classification attempts were characterized by unwarranted and unprofessional assumptions, inadequate evidence and, in some cases, sheer guess work. Greenberg introduced the procedure of "mass comparison" of language vocabularies. These included basic lexical items in major form classes such as nouns, verbs, adjective, etc as well as bound morphemes or affixes performing grammatical functions. Such lexical items are referred to as cognates. It is now common knowledge in historical or comparative linguistics that if languages show striking similarities in both form and meaning in basic vocabulary items technically referred to as cognates - in this way excluding loan words - it is concluded that such languages are related. This is the tenet of genetic classification. The higher the level of cognacy (i.e. the similarity in form and meaning), between or among languages, the closer the relationship is between or among the languages. Lower degrees of cognacy, on the other hand, reflect more distant relationships among languages. Predictably, completely unrelated languages show only a very little random similarity, if any, and this is attributed to coincidence or perhaps to borrowing.

6.11.1.1 Greenberg's analysis itself

Before we examine Greenberg's analysis, itself, we should perhaps state the number of languages spoken in Africa. According to Bernd Heine and Derek Nurse in their introduction to the volume *African Languages* (2000), Grimes (ed. 1996) put the number at 2,035, though this number is by no means fixed, since some languages are still being 'discovered' while others are disappearing. This number excludes Arabic, Malagasy, Afrikaans, English, French, Spanish and Portuguese. Globally, according to Garry and Rubino (eds. 2001), there are "just over 6000" languages. Africa, south of the Sahara Desert, therefore, has just a little over one-third of the world's languages. Actually the number of languages spoken in Africa depends to a large extent on the distinction between **language** and **dialect** that individual researchers on this matter make. For a variety of reasons, usually political and external interest, clusters of dialects (eg the Efik-Ibibio and the Ejagham), (cf Essien 1987), have been classified as separate languages by 'splitters' (e.g. Cook, 1985, Williamson (cf. Williamson 1999, etc.). Unfortunately in nearly all African countries, including Nigeria, it is foreign linguists particularly from North America and Europe, who determine the number of languages spoken there. How altrustic or objective they are is anybody's guess. But this quotation taken from Heine & Nurse (2003:3) speaks for itself:

Linguists who try to deal with this welter of languages are often referred to as 'splitters' or 'lumpers'. Splitters tend to regard 'varieties' as distinct languages, thus boosting the 2000 while lumpers treat varieties as just dialects, reducing the number.

Greenberg divided languages of Africa into four major families commonly referred to as phyla (phylum for one). These are Afro-Asiatic, Nilo-Saharan, Niger-Kodofanian and Khosian.

Let us briefly examine these phyla beginning with the Niger-Kodofanian. Greenberg regarded Kodofanian and Niger-Congo as two related families. He recognized five groups of languages as making up Kodofanian. He subdivided these into two major sub-classifications one sub-classification consisting of one called Tumtum and the other four with no details of this class.

For Greenberg, Niger-Congo is made up of six branches, viz: West Atlantic, Mande, Gur, Kwa, Benue-Congo, and Adamawa-Eastern.

According to Greenberg one of the traits of Niger-Congo morphology is nominal classification by pair of affixes, one singular and the other plural. The Bantu noun prefixes are fairly typical of this classification. So we have in Bantu the pair *mu-singular, ba-plural* for objects, the objects that come in pairs, though the class meanings are by no means always clear. While these affixes appear as prefixes in Bantu and the languages of the Benue-Congo in general as well as in other subfamilies, sometimes they appear as suffixes as in many of the Gur languages and sometimes as both simultaneously in some of the Gur languages and sparodically elsewhere. Of the Eastern languages, the Adamawa branch exhibits suffixes, the Eastern branch some uncertain traces of prefixes and suffices for Mondunga and Mba. Greenberg has observed the drift in Niger-Congo in the direction of simplification of the nominal class system. This is said to have reached its apogee or climax in Mande and the Kwa languages in which the affixes, have been entirely lost and an isolating system results. Greenberg concludes that while the presence of these affixes provides important evidence for a genetic relationship with the Niger-Congo family, absence of them does not prove lack of connection

This simplification is going on gradually and imperceptibly even in the more Bantu-like languages in the Benue-Congo, as observed by Essien (1983, 1990).

Another characteristic of Niger-Congo Languages is verbal extension, described by Essien (1990:107) in relation to Bantoid languages in this way:

> There are certain affixes-mostly suffixes - connected with verbs, which extend as it were, the verb root (or sometimes radicals) such that the resultant form is capable of taking on its inflectional affixes (e.g. those of concord, tense,

aspect, etc) just like the root from which it is derived.

This is why Williamson and Blench (2000:10) say "verbs commonly end in suffixes that modify their meaning and often their valency, [i.e. the number of objects they take] thus creating causatives, reciprocals and the like. In a language like Ibibio, they include reflexives and relatives. One of the major conclusions that Greenberg arrived at, according to Welmers, is the inclusion of Bantu Languages with a number of other languages to the northwest of Bantu in a Benue-Congo branch of the Niger-Congo phylum.

The other phyla as already stated are:

(a) Nilo-Saharan phylum: Of the four Greenberg's phyla, Nilo-Saharan is probably the least widely accepted. According to Greenberg, it consists of six branches as follows:

   1. Songhai
   2. Saharan: (a)Kanuri, Kanembu; (b) Teda, Daza; (c) Zaghawa, Beti.
   3. Maban: Maba, Runga, Mimi (of Nachtigal, Mime(of Gaude-froy-Demombynes)
   4. Fur
   5. Chari-Nile

6. Coman: Koma, Ganza, uduk, Gule, Gumuz, Mao.

According to Bender (2000:51), Nilo-Saharan languages are spoken in significant numbers in 15 African countries: Eritrea, Ethiopia, Kenya, Tanzania, Uganda, Sudan, Egypt, Chad, Central African Republic, Nigeria, Benin, Burkina Faso, Mali, in addition to 'spillovers' in Algeria: The greatest variety in terms of genetic classification are found in Chad, the Sudan and Ethiopia. It is difficult to say how many Nilo-Saharan languages are spoken in Africa because of the thorny question of how to separate languages from dialects, the same situation that is applicable to Niger-Congo languages. Bender (2000) gives 108, because he lumped a number of dialects into languages while Grimes (1996) as a splitter of languages gives 195.

As in the case of Niger-Congo languages, Greenberg also carried out mass comparison of basic vocabulary items and the morphologies of these languages. In particular he compared personal pronouns in their singular and plural forms, demonstratives, relatives, locative, and accusative cases as well as adjectives and common suffixation in verbs. In fact he gives a list of forty-eight grammatical areas of evidence of the similarities among the six branches which are rather complicated at this introductory level.

6.12 Afroasiatic

What is now known as Afroasiatic (or Afrosian or Afrasan) was first introduced by Greenberg (1963:50) after he had rejected earlier scholars' names like Hamito-Semitic for the family of languages found both in Africa and Asia. By this name Greenberg also rejected the theories of racially mixed peoples' languages suggested by Fitzgerald (1964:127) and Meinhof (1899). From Greenberg (P.49), this is what Meinhof himself has said, "Bantu is a mixed language, so to speak, descended of a Hamitic father and a Negro mother."

According to Hayword (2000:74), Afrosiatic is probably the least controversial of Greenberg's four phyla. Long before Greenberg (1950a), a core of what is now referred to as Afrosiatic had been recognized and subsequent to that publication, there has been no serious suggestion that the Afrosiatic concept should be called into question. There has been no universal agreement either about the internal structure of the phylum or complete unanimity about the membership of every language group proposed, but regarding the overall Afrosiatic hypothesis there has been wide satisfaction. There are some interesting features of this phylum. First, it is the only phylum that includes some languages spoken exclusively outside the continent of Africa. Secondly, in terms of history of mankind, it is incontrovertible that some of the earliest and greatest human achievements have been accomplished by civilizations founded by Afroasitic peoples. The Egyptians, Assyrians, Phoeicians, Jews, Arabs, to mention only some whose architecture, mathematics and astronomy, medical practice, religions, philosophies and laws have contributed so vastly to human development and progress, have been speakers of Afroasiatic languages.

Thirdly, Afroasiatic languages have great time-depths. In the case of Semitic languages, there are written specimens of languages going back 4,000 years- very ancient languages indeed. According to Hayward, the differences, however, between these and any 20th Century Semitic language are considerably less than that between either of them and say, any modern Chadic or Omotic language. There are, of course, cognate forms and structures – without which there would not be substance at all to the Afroasitic Hypothesis – but the purpose in making these comparisons is to draw attention to extreme antiquity of Afroasiatic. 8,000BC has been assigned to a proto- Afroasitic by Diakonoff (1988:25), according to Hayward.

According to Greenberg the Afroasiatic has five branches namely (1) Semitic, (2) Berber, (3) Ancient Egyptian, (4) Cushitic, (5) Chad. But the latest classification by Hayward (2000:74) gives 6 as follows: (1) Chadic, (2) Berber (3) Egyptian (4) Semitic, (5) Cushitic and (6) Omotic.

Geographically Afroasiatic languages spread within Africa largely to the north of the continent. It is only in Tanzania that Afrosatic languages are spoken North of the

Equator. Clearly Arabic is spoken in North-Africa and Asia and Hebrew in Asia (Middle East) as a Semitic language while the Cushitic ones are spoken mostly in East Africa. According to Grimes (1996) Afroasiatic comprises 371 extant linguistic varieties.

6.12.1 A run-down of the Afroasiatic families

Berber: Four main groups of languages and dialect clusters are distinguishable as spoken today. These are:

1. Varieties spoken from north-western Morocco through northern Algeria and Tunisia into Libya. They include Tashelhit (3,000); Tamazight (3,000); Tarifit (2,000) and Kabyle (3,074).

2. Isolated varieties spoken in Libya and in the Siwa Oasis in Egypt; they include: Awjilah (2,000) and Siwa (5).

3. Sahara-Sahelian varieties spoken by communities scattered across a largely dessert territory taking in parts of Southern Algeria, Niger, Mali and Burkina Faso. Tamahaq to the North of the range and Tamajeg further south belong here.

4. Zenaga (23) living to the south-west of the Berber range in part of Mauritania speak a distinct variety.

Chadic
According to Newman (1993:253) there are about 140 Chadic languages spreading in three directions from Lake Chad, from which the family takes its name, and are spoken in parts of Nigeria, Chad, Cameroun, Central African Republic and Niger. The best known and most widely spoken Chadic language is Hausa. Given millions of second language speakers, Hausa is probably the largest African language, excluding Arabic.

Egyptian
This family is said to have had 42 millennia of written records until it died in the 14th – century. In terms of time the Egyptian family has been divided into Old Egyptian (3,100-2000 BC), Middle Egyptian (2,000 – 1, 1300BC), Late Egyptian, Hieratic, Demotic, Coptic, etc. Egyptian, which are associated with Literary and Graphic matters, rather than with linguistic features per se.

Semitic
This is said to be the most studied and best known branch of the Afroasiatic phylum. It is said to exhibit some 50 distinct varieties. Most authorities seem to recognize three subfamilies namely North-east, North-West and South. Arabic, in one opinion and analysis, which is spoken partly in Africa, belongs to the North-east. Other Semitic languages are Aramaic spoken during the first six centuries

of the Christian era, Hebrew and Amharic, the National language of Ethiopia, to mention a few.

Cushitic
This family is said to consist of six groups of languages some of which are very distinct from each other. These are:

1. *Northern Cushitic* containing a single language Bedawi/Beja (1,148) spoken in an area overlapping portions of Sudan, Egypt and Eritrea.

2. *Central Cushitic* referring to the Agaw languages, a well-defined group of varieties spoken in North-Western Ethiopia and Eritrea.

3. *Highland East Cushitic*. This constitutes another quite close-knit cluster, whose speakers generally live in the mountainous areas of Central Southern Ethiopia.

4. *Lowland East Cushitic*. This comprises 3 distinct subgroups

(i) Northern Sub-group consisting of closely related Saho and Afar, (ii) the Ormoid Subgroup comprising Ovomo (Proper) Spoken in Kenya and along the borders of Sudan and Tigrai zone of Ethiopia and Konsoid, a dialect chain west of the southern Rift Valley of Ethiopia; (iii) Omo-tara comprising eastern and western divisions. They include languages like Kenyan Rendille and Boni, numerous varieties of Somali spoken in Somalia, Djiobouti, eastern Ethiopia and north-Eastern Kenya.

5. Duallay – representing a linguistic chain in the Wayt'o valley, to the west of Konsoid (cf. 4ii) above.

6. Southern Cushitic Languages are spoken mostly in Tanzania where they are represented by the Iraqw cluster comprising Iragw, Gorowa and Burunge, etc.

Omotic
According to Hayward, (2000) scholars recognize the existence of two major groups of languages, namely North and South Omotic subfamilies. South Omotic comprises Aari, Hamer –Banna, Karo and Dime. North Omotic falls into 2 divisions viz Dizoid and Gonga -Gimojan, each with its own cluster of languages.

6.12.2 What evidence is there for Greenberg's Afroasiatic classification?

Before Greenberg, there were spurious hypotheses about the relationship of languages first referred to as Afroasiatic by Greenberg (1963) himself. After the misconceptions and misanalyses of earlier scholars like Carl Meinhof (1912) M. Delafosse, etc believing in the mixture of languages and / or typological consideration, Greenberg dismissed such spurious hypothesis in this confident way.

> However, any theory which at once harmonizes with the flattering view of the general predominance of the Caucasoid over Negroid types under all cultural circumstances in Africa and which involves a fairly constant correlation of linguistic, cultural and physical traits over a long period of time, must almost inevitably turn out to be false.

In other words, before Greenberg, there were considerations to classifying African languages other than linguistics.

For the Afroasiatic hypothesis, Greenberg resorted to mass comparison of basic vocabulary item among these languages as he did in other phyla. Below is a small portion of his Afroasiatic comparative word list:

1. *antelope*   Ch: Ankwe (i) jiri : 'road antelope'
      Buduma (2) ŋgəi : 'gezelle'
      Logone (2) garia
      Cushitic: Beja (N) garuwa; Sidamo (E) gedimo;
      Iraqw (s) gwarehi : 'dik-dik

2. *arrow*   Chad: Bede (Ngzizim) (1) salo: 'cut'
      Gulfei (2) si:l; Buduma (2) hal 'to stab',
      Balda (4) zala, Mofu (4) sellam;
      Gisiga (4) suil 'knife'
      Barein (9) saalu 'knife'

Cushitic: Beja (N) sal 'sharp, 'pointed'
      Kamir (c) sil 'knife',
      Quara (c) selau 'sharp'

He also examined morphological characteristics: This was quite in the right direction. For as observed by Hayward (2000:86):

    It is generally agreed that shared morphology is the surest proof of genetic relatedness. Phonemes have no meaning in themselves and their organization into systems and their phonetic realizations are all too prone to areal influences. Lexicon, moreover, is always open to infiltration by borrowing. Such problems are far less common with morphology.

For the Afroasiatic phylum, then these are some of the aspects of shared morphology initiated by Greenberg (1963) and complemented by others like Hayward (2000).

6.12.3 Morphology
6.12.3.1 Personal pronouns

According to Hayward, there is substantial agreement on the main points, in particular in pronominal forms, though Omotic languages may show less of these. The clearest similarities in forms are found in possessive determiners and object complement functions. Ehret (1995) has the following reconstruction cited in Hayward (2000:88) referred to as primary series.

1sg 'me, my': E: *-ay; P – S: ii, * ya', * - ni (as object complement).

B: -i, - i-n; P-C: *yi - *yu - * ya; Ch:wa, ni; O:yi-n, P-AA: i-Yi

2SG 'you, your': P.E: m. **-ku, f. * * - ki; P-S: m. * - ka, f. * - ki ; B: m –f, f (k) m; P. C: m. *ku, f. *ki; Ch:m. ka, f. kim; O: no obvious cognates; P. AA:m: * ku, *ka, f. * ki

3sg ' him, his, her' : P.E:m * * -su, **-sr; P – S:m. *šu, f. B: m. & f. – s, P.C: m. *? i-su (u) - *?i –sa (a), f. *?i –sii; Ch :m . ši, f. ta; O: m iz-n, f. iž-n; P-AA: m. & f. *si, *isi.

/p/ 'us, our': P-E: m: * * - ina; P.-s: * - na- * -nu - *ni; B:ng, P.C: * na - *nu-ni, *?ina – etc; Ch: na; O: in.

2p/ 'you' : P –E: ** - kina; P-S: m. * Kumu, f. * - kina \; B: M.-un, f. unt; O: no P. C: *kun (V) – kin (V); Ch: kun; no obvious cognates; P-AA: * kuuna.

3p/ 'them' : P-E: **-sina; P-S:m. *-šumu, f. *šina; B:m.-sn, f. snt; P-C: * ?isun V - *?1-sin V; Ch: * sun; O: iš-n; P-AA: *su - * usu.

6.12.3.2 Case markers

Case marking is found in Afroasiatic languages. Cushitic, Berber and Egyptian case systems are said to be similar or identical. Within the Proto-Afroasiatic system, there is a so-called basic nominal form referred to as absolutive and it is most generally characterized by a final *-a. According to Hayward (2000:88), "cross-linguistically, the core role of the absolutive is to mark the head of an NP functioning as the direct object of a verb".

On the other hand, there is a nominative form * - u, found in unfocussed subject NPs. But some modification need to be made. First a distinct nominative often occurs only in the masculine gender. Second, within Cushitic a nominative in – i̱ is far more widespread than one in – u̱. It is suggested by Hetzron (1980:16-17) that the * - i̱ nominative is a Cushitic innovation. The Egyptian evidence for the nominative consists mainly of non-functional relic labial-velar glide morpheme e.g. **haf3aw (<** haf3atu): 'snake', *haaruw 'Horns', *masdiw 'enemy' but it survives for phonological reasons as a vowel in certain monosyllables, e.g. P-E: * *nibu: 'lord; the absolutive in-a is best preserved in certain syntactic constructions based on deverbal nominalizations.

Chadic shows no obvious traces of this system. On the other hand, the Omoto cluster and Gimira of Omotic have a case system of the type described, and masculine nouns do mark the nominative with an-i̱ suffix, while feminines indicate the nominative case with – a̱, though this is not identical to the absolutive.

The form often referred to as genitive is more appropriately called 'oblique', for in addition to indicating possessive relationships, it often also serves to mark a noun as an appositional complement. We shall not go into this.

6.12.3.3 Verbal Morphemes

There are also what are referred to (cf. Hayward 2000:90) as conjugational features of the verb or better still what I would simply call verbal morphemes that Afroasiatic languages have been shown to have in common to help justify them as belonging to one phylum. This is better seen in the aspectual prefixal marking of perfect/imperfect as exemplified by an imperfect paradigm of the Arabic Verb: 'write'

1sg: ? – aktub – u, 2m. sg: t-aktub-u, 3m.sg: y-aktub-u, 3 f.sg: t-aktub-u, 1pl n-aktub-u, etc.

The perfect paradigm in modern Semitic does not have these prefixes, but in an earlier stage of the family, both perfect and imperfect were marked prefixally in Aktadjan, a Semitic language. Such a conjugation pattern is found in Berber and in certain verbs in Cushitic languages. Egyptian can boast of another archaic verb pattern known as stative conjugation which has its reflexes in Semitic Atkadian.

6.12.4 Word formation processes

Afroasiatic languages are known to have word-formation processes of creating new words from existing ones by means of affixes, often in combination. Verbs so derived differ from their bases in terms of syntactic arguments structure, voice, and the like. For example, a transitivising/ causative (cf. Hayward 2000:93), is found in all six families, eg. E: *si-min- 'establish', compare *man- 'to be stable'; S- Amharic: as- wässädä 'he caused to take; compara wässädä 'he took', B: ss-xdn 'cause to work, compare xdm ' work' ss-isin: in form', compare isin 'know', C- Sidamo: ra? - is- 'bail (tr)', compare ra? - 'boil' (int); Ch - Ngizim: dəɓs 'hide', daas - 'pour (tr) through a narrow opening; O- Aari: lang-s 'tire (tr)', compare lang- 'feel tired', Gamo: gup-iss- 'cause to jump', compare gupp- 'jump'.

Other wide spread derivational affixes are: m- - m, n- and t – v – t, associated variously with notions of reflexivity, reciprocity, and /or intransitivising /passivizing formations.

6.13 Khosian

The Khoisan languages, for a long time labelled and commonly known as 'Bushman' and 'Hottentot' languages represent the widely accepted but controversial hypothesis that they are the smallest of the four language phyla in Africa, according to Greenberg (1963). In the past, the no. of languages and dialects might have exceeded100, but today only 30 Khoisan languages are still extant, according to Güldermann and Vossen (2000:99).

According to Greenberg, Khoisan is a convenient term for the compound of <u>Khoi</u>, the Hottentot's name for themselves and their name for the Bushmen, S<u>a</u>n. They are culturally distinguished: the Hottentots being cattle-raising while the Bushmen are hunters and food-gatherers, though these are no basis for genetic classification. Greenberg credits this name to Schapera in 1930 but Güldermann & Vossen (2000:102) credit it to Leonhardt Schuize two years earlier in 1928, both of whom were anthropologists. Greenberg identified the languages of the 'Bushmen' and the Hottentonts in southern Africa as well as two languages in East Africa Sandawe and Hatsa as belonging to the Khoisan phylum. These four (groups of) languages have clicks in their phonologies. There are, of course neighbouring Bantu languages with clicks which do not belong with Khoisan languages even in Greenberg's classification. This notwithstanding, Greenberg has said this:

In phonology, the most important evidence of the basically Khoisan relationships of Hottentot is the frequency of click sounds and the essential part they play in the phonology of the language.

According to Güldermann and Vossen (2000:99) geographically, the majority of modern Khoisan languages are spoken over much of Botswana and Namibia. There are also pockets of speakers in adjacent regions: in southern Angola and Zambia, Western Zimbabwe as well in northern South Africa. Formerly, probably the larger part of present-day South Africa was Khoisan-speaking. Two isolated languages also considered to be of Khoisan stock are located in distant Tanzania, as was already observed by Greenberg.

The Khoisan characteristics

(1)   A phonology which has a frequency of click sounds and the essential part they play in the phonology of the language, as pointed out above. Although it is not the case that any language which has clicks is Khoisan, it is, however, the case that all Khoisan languages have clicks. According to Greenberg, clicks play a fundamental part in root formation in South African Khoisan languages. According to him clicks occur only initially in nouns, verbs and adjectives.

As in the cases of the other languages, mass comparison of basic vocabulary was carried out by Greenberg. In addition, he did a comparative morphological analysis. Resemblances were discovered in the presence of grammatical gender in both East African and South-African Khoisan languages, particularly between Sundawe in East Africa and Hottentot in South Africa.

Sundawe has a number of morphological features which resemble those of the South African group, particularly in pronouns, according to Greenberg. First person <u>tsi</u> is equivalent to <u>ti</u> of Hottentot and Naron and <u>č</u> i of Hierciware. The third person feminine pronoun <u>sa</u> is cognate to the -<u>s</u> of Hottentot and -<u>sg</u> of Naron. Common gender singular <u>e</u> resembles tha-<u>i</u> nominative -<u>e</u> accusative of the Hottentot. Similarly, in Hottentot and Naron, a demonstrative functions as a base for the 3rd person pronouns. It is the form <u>ha</u>- which means 'he, she, it' throughout the Northern and Southern Bushman groups. The masculine singular affix- <u>we</u> appended to it to form <u>ha</u> -<u>we</u> 'he' may be plausibly compared to the -<u>b</u> masculine of Hottentot and Naron. In its elements and formation Sandawe <u>ha-we</u> thus completely parallels Naron <u>xa-ba</u>. Similarly, <u>ha-su</u>, <u>he-su</u> 'she' resembles Naron xa-sa.

These observations, and many more we cannot go into because of time constraint, taken from Greenberg himself are just what we expect in genetically related languages.

6.13.1 Post-Greenberg classification

Although Greenberg did a seminal job classifying African languages substantially departing from earlier classifiers like Meinhof whose method was primarily typological, according to Williamson & Blench (2000:16ff) Greenberg's work was initially controversial but was gradually accepted by most scholars. Mukarovsky (1976-7), a student of Westerman presented an overview of the Niger-Congo without using evidence from Kordofanian, Mande, the Wolof-Server-Fulfude group, Ijoid and Adamawa-Eastern for unstated reasons.

Bennet and Sterk (1977) proposed a major reclassification of Niger-Congo, based mainly on lexicostatistics and lexical innovations. Their argument was that Kordofanian with relatively few lexical cognates and Mande, with its complete loss of noun class system, should be treated as the first families to break off from the rest. This yielded a three-way initial split. The next to split from the rest was West Atlantic supported by lexicostatistical sampling. The rest of the families were treated as Central Niger-Congo, splitting into North and South. Niger-Congo comprised Gur and Adamawa-Eastern, possibly with Kru. South Central Niger-Congo comprised Western and Eastern, possibly with Ijo. In 1989, with the publication of *The Niger-Congo Languages* edited by Bendor-Samuel, in which a modification of Bennet and Sterk's proposal was presented as a working hypothesis (cf. Williamson 1989) it was observed that an important change was made to Greenberg's hypothesis, namely 'Niger-Congo' replaced 'Niger-Kordofanian' as the overall name for the phylum. But the initial three-way branching was retained. So was the next branching with minor modifications between Atlantic and Volta-Congo and Ijoid tentatively then forming a 3rd branch. Volta-Congo was presented with a more conservative flat array comprising Kru, New Kwa ('Western South Central Niger-Congo'), New Benue-Congo (Eastern South Central Niger-Congo'), North Central Niger-Congo') and tentatively, Dogon, which had been removed from Gur. A system of nomenclature proposed by Stewart was adopted in which the direct ancestors of Bantu, from Niger-Congo to Benue-Congo, all had compound names ending in -Congo' while lower nodes naming relatively closely related groups ended in '-oid'.

Williamson and Blench (2000:18) have given a genealogical tree for the internal structure of Niger-Congo.

Williamson and Blench (2000) have done a good job giving a rundown of the general structural characteristics of the Niger-Congo languages in families, groups and subgroups. Let us begin with Kordofanian family believed to be the earliest to have split.

Linguistic features of Kordofanian
Noun Class: Full/reduced/absent; incorporated old prefixes, new prefixes.

Verbal Extensions: widespread.

Pronouns: Inclusive/exclusive.

Sentence word order: SVO (Tegem Sov); Prepositions.

Noun phrase (NP): N +Gen; N + Poss (Tegem Poss + N; N + Adj; N + Num, N + Dem.

Features of Mande
Noun Classes: Remnant; remodelled by affixes, initial consonant mutation unconditioned; tone alternation marks singular/Plural (e.g. Sembla).

Verbal extensions: Not generally, but **Bɔbɔ** has causative, intransitive.

Pronouns: Alienable/inalienable, inclusive/exclusive common. **b** has a separate feminine.

Sentence word order: SMOVA; Propositions/Post positions. *NP*: Gen +N; Poss +N; N + Adj; Dem + N, N + Dem; N + Plural.

Linguistic features of Atlantic
Noun class: Full; original prefixes; weakened, renewed affixes by suffixes, or augments; initial consonant mutation grammatically conditioned Verbal.

Extensions: Widespread.

Pronouns: Inclusive /exclusive common.

Sentence word order: SVOA; Prepositions.

NP: N + Gen (Gen + N in Sua); N + Num; N + Dem.

Linguistic features of Ijoid

Noun Classes: Remnant; a -marks plural nouns preceded by modifier, some initial vowels, new human suffixes.

Verbal Extensions: Few, mostly new formations.

Pronouns: Inalienable/alienable traces. New gender system, always distinguishing feminine from masculine, sometimes masculine from neuter, in singular, reflected in determiners.

Sentence word order: SAOV, Postpositions.

NP: Gen + N; Poss + N; Adj + N; Num + N; Dem + N, N + Definite.

Linguistic features of Dogon

Noun classes: Remnant: no prefixes: human nouns take distinct plural suffix.

Verbal Extensions: Few, mostly new formations.

Pronouns: One basic set with object, possessive and 'embedded' sets derived.

Sentence word order: SAOVM.

NP: N + Poss; N + Adj; N + Pl; N + Num; N +Dem; N + Definite.

Linguistic features of Kru
Noun Classes: Remnant, Suffixes or final vowel change in the Pl; some concord in the NP.

Verbal extension: Causative, benefactive, inchoative, instrumental, dative, locative, passive.

Pronouns: Human/non-human common, fem. In 2nd and 3rd sign in Niaboua and Wobé.

Sentence word order: SVOA, SMOVA; Postpositions

NP: Gen + N; Poss + N; N +Adj; N+ Dem; N + Num; N + Definite.

Linguistic features of Gur
Noun Classes: Full/reduced; normally suffixes, Eastern Grusi (Tem) has survivals of older prefixes in some common nouns.
Verbal Extensions: Widespread.

Pronouns: Reconstructed with consonant plus varying vowels.

Sentence word order: SVO, SMOV; Postpositions (one prep. 'with').

NP: Gen + N; Poss + N; N + Adj; N + Num; N + Dem.

Linguistic features of Adamawa-Ubangi

Noun Classes: Reduced Remnant, suffixes in some groups; if concord markers, prefixed to postposed modifiers.

Verbal Extensions: A few including iterative, intensive, benefactive and causative.

Pronouns: Sometimes inclusive/exclusive. 2nd sing often # mo (as in Kru; Serufo, and Kasern (Gur), contrasting with normal 1st sing # mi.

Sentence word order: SVO, SMOV; Prepositions.

NP: N + Gen (Duru Gen + N); N + Adj (often Adj + N in Ubangi); N + Num; N + Dem.

Linguistic features of Kwa

Noun classes: Full (Ega)/reduced/remnant; prefixes, some plural suffixes, initial consonant mutation, often phonologically conditioned.

Verbal extensions: At least causative and reflexive/reciprocal.

Pronouns: Independent, subject, object, possessive. Animate/non- animate common in 3rd person.

Sentence word order: SMVOA; postpositions

NP: Gen + N; Poss + N; N + Adj; N + Num; N + Dem; N + Definite.

Linguistic features West-Benue-Congo

Noun Class: Full (Gade) reduced (Edoid/remnant (Yoruba); Prefixes.

Verbal Extensions: Edoid has a number (often indicating plurality) and Igboid many, most of which are new developments.

Pronouns: Independent, subject, objective, possessive.

Sentence word order: SMVOA, SVMOA, Prepositions

NP: N + Gen; N + Poss; N + Adj; N + Num; N + Dem; N + Definite.

Linguistic features of Cross River

Noun Class: Full (Some upper cross)/reduced (Abuan)/none (Gokana).

Verbal Extensions: Various, often coalescing with verb root, often indicate plurality.
Pronouns: Independent, subject, object, possessive.

Sentence word order: SMVOA, SVMOA, Prepositions.

NP: N + Gen; N + Poss; Adj + N, N + Adj; N + Num, N + Dem; N + Definite.

Linguistic features of Bantoid

Noun Classes: Full (Bantu/reduced (Vute)/remnant (Mambila).

Verbal Extensions: Widely attested.

Pronouns: 3rd person concord with noun classes.

Sentence word order: SMVOA, SVMOA; Prepositions.

NP: N + Gen; N + Poss; N + Adj; N + Num, N + Dem; N + Definite.

6.14 Nilo-Saharan

As we have pointed out early, of the four phyla hypothesized by Greenberg (1963) Nilo-Saharan is the least widely accepted. While Greenberg divided it into 6 'branches' viz, Songhai, Sharan, Maban, Fur, Chari-Nile and Coman, Bender (2000) following the principle of historical-comparative methodology, which regards innovations the best evidence for grouping languages, divides the phylum into 3 independent branches labeled as A, B, K (Songay, Saharan and Kuliak respectively with a fourth branch C referred to as S.C (Satellite-Core). This latter branch makes up [C, D, F, G, H] as 'Satelites' and [E, I, J, L] as core.

In summary, Bender says this:

> To summarise the structure shown about A, B, and K (Songay, Saharan and Kuliak respectively) are independent branches of Nilo-Saharan, with S-C (Satellite-Core) being a fourth branch. Within S-C, there are six independent branches, C, D, F, G, H, Core (Maban, Fur, Central Sudanic, Berta, Kunama

and Core). Core consists of four families E, I, J, L (East Sudanic, Koman, Gumuz and Kadu).

An interesting point worth pointing out is the lingering question as to whether Nilo-Saharan is infact a phylum or as Bender (2000:60) puts it 'just a collection of unrelated groups?

Bender (ibid) argues that what characterizes Nilo-Saharan as a phylum "is not a collection of typological attributes such as monosyllabism or tonality, but rather a collection of lexical and grammatical morphemes reconstructable to a common ancestor by the comparative method". It can also be shown that it is separate from what is reconstructed for the other... established phyla-Niger-Congo, Afroasiatic and Khosian. According to Bender, it is only in the case of Afroasiatic is there a comparable body of work which allows this kind of separation to be made. Niger-Congo and Nilo-Saharan are said to be probably a super-phylum. In that case the task here is to show that these two are separated by innovations. In the case of Nilo-Saharan, 46 retentives are established and these are found in the areas of pronouns, deictic pattern near/far or to /away singular/plural ali-ila, copula y (E), verbal negations, verbal transitive/causative or factive ('cause someone to do'), etc.

Bender also gives a tentative analysis of innovating languages of the phylum to justify the figure presented earlier to show how genetically related languages can exhibit similarities in innovations. In this way he set off-the S-C core group from the rest, though they together still belong to the same phylum, at least in theory.

6.15 Afrosiatic (AA)

According to Hayward (2000:82), AA is a hypothesis based on the linguistic facts that are available. And these facts point to the genetic relationship of the six families discussed earlier. But as pointed out by Hayward, whenever similarities are observed between languages, they have to be valued in ways that will disentangle signals of genuine shared linguistic parentage from those that are merely typological or traits resulting from a shared geography, factors that deluded classifiers of African languages before Greenberg. The only admissible evidence is where similarities of meaning or function are accompanied by regular pattern of similarity in form, that is, cross-linguistic sound-meaning correspondences which are so iterable as to lead to predictability. And this is the principle of the comparative method, which is mostly post-Greenberg. Greenberg, as clearly admitted by him, used the 'mass comparison method, rather than the comparative method, to establish the cannon of AA languages. Although this methodology clearly avoided the reliance on typological features, it does not invoke the rigour of the principle of cross-linguistic sound-meaning correspondence and cannot therefore make prediction falling short of true theoretical status. In addition, it lacks a filter for rejecting unrelated 'look alikes' nor any means of recognising highly dissimilar, albeit cognate, items.

So the comparative method at the morphological level was viewed as 'the surest proof of genetic relationship after Greenberg and indeed enhances Greenberg's mass comparative method' in establishing ultimate relatedness of languages. In this case of AA, the method has been used to investigate personal pronouns, case markers, conjugational or verbal inflections, plural formative, verbal derivation or verbal extension, and gender and gender markers.

In furtherance of the AA hypothesis through the lexicon and phonology, Hayward (2006:94) gives examples of re-constructed lexical items for P-AA, some of which are disputed. We repeat them here below, for whatever they are worth.

*ba 'not be there, neg. (Eh.2), *bak- 'strike, squeeze (O &S. '94) + O – Gamo bak – 'strike'); * pir-'fly (V)' (EH. 51); * fir-'flow' bear fruit' (EH. 85;....')

His general comments are more useful at this point in time, so I repeat them below:

> Regarding consonants, the preceding reconstructions involve quite straightforward sound correspondences. P-AA in the first example above is reconstructed on the basis of E: b:c: *b : Ch: *b : No: *b. But P. AA seems to have had a rich consonant inventory, just as many of its

descendants do today. There is a general agreement that obstruents must have been organized in triads contrasting glottalized with plain voiced and voiceless series not only for most places of articulation but also for certain other articulatory parameters, e.g. among lateral obstruents, sibilants and labialized velars. A gutural series comprising pharyngeals and laryngeals is also always postulated for the proto-language. During the various family evolutions, and at every lower level, the hypothesized inventories have been whittled down as a result of numerous mergers. The details of these events have not been agreed upon, however... Large-scale, phylum-wide comparison stimulates the imagination and serves to inject a sense of purpose into the AA enterprise, but the most pressing need continues to be that of detailed and extensive lexical reconstruction within the constituent families.

6.16 Khosian
Phonetics and phonology
Types of sounds, phonological system and typology
Following Güldermann & Vossen (2000:105), the safest thing to say about the Khoisan phylum even after Greenberg is that the Khoisan sound systems are not only unique in Africa but figure among the most complex in the world. To be sure clicks constitute the most prominent of

the complexities of these systems. But the languages also possess other rare cross-linguistic features not found in other African phyla.

One of the post-Greenberg contributions are more detailed descriptions of the varieties of clicks given by Trial 1985, 1993, 1997. In this regard, a distinction is made between click 'in flux' and 'effux'. This is how Güldermann and Vossen describe the distinction:

In the production of the so-called suction mechanism, the tongue is moved against the roof of the mouth creating a closure in the oral cavity. The central tongue body is then lowered while the blade and back of the tongue maintain the closure. Thus the pressure of the air trapped in the cavity decreases. Then the front closure is released, the air rushing in being responsible for the loud noise typical of clicks. The way the anterior tongue body is manipulated determines the type of the click influx. There are five such influxes, commonly symbolized and labeled as follows: ⊙- bilabial, | = dental, ! = alveolar, ǂ = palatal, and ǁ = lateral. However, the terms are inadequate for an exhaustive description and explanation of the internal relations between the different types (Trail 1993, 1995). The click efflux or accompaniment is shaped by the manner of release of the posterior closure. Here the diversity of types is even greater (cf. Ladefoged and Trail 1994) and Khoisanists still diverge in their description and representation. The combinations of various influx and efflux types sometimes lead to excessively large click inventories.

6.16.1 Typological and areal classification of African languages

As we have seen above, genetic classification of languages has to do with the tracing of languages to the source or parent at differing levels – phylum, family, subfamily, branch, group or subgroup based on cognates and morphological correspondences. As we have seen earlier Greenberg used mass comparison of the basic vocabulary items from various languages to come to the conclusions that he did and brought some refinements through the comparative method.

In the cases of typological and areal classifications, no attempt is made to trace similarities in structure to a parent source or proto-language, i.e. a language assumed to have existed at some time in the past. In typological classification, similarities are not based on properties of language which may reflect historical connection or contacts such as kinds of tonal system, the presence of particular morphological features, word order in sentences, or vocalic or consonantal systems. On the other hand, areal classification is based on diffusion of linguistic features, allowing one to establish the existence of linguistic areas, for example, the Balkans, South India, or Africa itself or same regions of Africa-for example the syntactic condition of tense/aspect allomorphs which we have discussed in 6.10.1.

6.16.2 Typological classification

According to Creissels (2000:231), when linguistic typology started in the 19th, its aim was to account for the structural diversity of languages by classifying them into a small number of types. In such classifications, each language taken as a whole was considered as belonging to a particular language type. However, modern research has made it clear that typology must begin with establishing types of structures in the individual subsystems that constitute a language, and not types of languages, since two languages may have the same type of structure in certain domains but different types of structures in other domains. Linguistic typology can be carried out from the phonological, morphological and syntactic levels. But for time limitations, let us focus on morphosyntactic features and here I have found the work of Creissels (2000:232ff) very useful.

Creissels has given five working hypothesis, which according to him are widely accepted in current work on language typology. They are repeated below:

1. Most natural languages syntactically have two major types of phrase, namely noun phrases (NP) and clauses.

2. The noun phrases (NP) consist of a noun (N) and a variable no. of modifiers.

3. With the possible exception of particular types of clause typically specialized in the expression of identification, existence, location or attribution of qualities, clauses result from the combination of a variable no. of NPs with a verb, and this construction can be at least partially analysed in terms of predicate-argument structure: the verb (predicate) assigns semantic roles to some of the NPs with which it combines (the arguments). (cf. 6.10.4).

4. The syntactic relations between the verb and the nominal terms of a clause are universally organized according to a contrast 'subject various (S)/(direct) object (O)/obliques (X)'. The notion of subject relies on syntactic mechanisms (relativisation, reflexive, pronoun control, etc.) that imply a hierarchy of the nominal terms of a clause: subject in a particular language can be defined as the formal type of relation with the verb characteristic of normal terms that, in the language in question, occupies the highest rank in this hierarchy. There are also syntactic mechanisms that reveal a variable degree of solidarity between the verb and the nominal term of the clause other than the subject (indexation, passivisation, etc.), and the (direct) object in a particular language can be defined as the

type of formal relation with the verb characteristic of normal terms other than subjects that, in the language in question, show the highest degree of solidarity with the verb in such mechanisms. With verbs representing actions involving an agent and patient, the subject typically represents the agent and the object typically represents the patient.

5. The genitive can be universally characterized as a noun phrase with the function of noun modifier in a construction that minimally specifies the semantic nature of the relation between the referent of the head noun and the referent of the noun phrase in modifier function.

While subject and direct object are viewed as universal notions, the same is not true of dative (or indirect) object: some languages have a particular type of syntactic relation distinct both from the (direct) object and from the obliques, typically associated with the semantic role of goal, but in many languages, the nominal term commonly called 'indirect object' is not clearly distinct from the obliques, and in some other languages (in particular in languages with double object constructions, which are very common in African languages) it may have the syntactic behaviour characteristic of (direct) objects.

6.16.3 Subject/Object

In addition to clause constituent order, the distinction between subject and object may involve case marking and indexation, and voice morphemes included in verb forms may modify the valence of the verb (intransitive/ transitive/ditransitive) and the semantic roles it assigns to is subject and/or objects).

In a majority of African languages, both subjects and objects are unmarked (except personal pronoun subjects and objects), that is they do not exhibit affixation, and position or prosodic contour distinguishing noun phrases in subject of object function from noun phrases quoted in isolation or citation form. This is particularly true of the overwhelming majority of Niger-Congo languages. However, in a number of Central Chadic languages, nouns functioning as objects are introduced by prepositions and case marked subject or objects as common in north-east Africa, in the Cushitic and Semitic branches of Afroasiatic and in certain branches of Nilo-Saharan.

Among the languages that have case marking system distinguishing the subject from the object, the most common type, both world-wide and Africa-wide, is that in which the subject is unmarked for case, while the object takes a particular case form, called accusative.

Another fairly common type globally is the ergative type of case marking, in which the object of transitive clauses and the subject of intransitive clauses are unmarked for case whereas the subject of transitive clauses takes a particular case form, generally referred to as ergative. No clear case of ergative case marking has been established in African languages, though a few African languages have been claimed to have ergative properties. This is consistent with strong predominance of the clause constituent order SVO among African Languages. It has been observed the ergative type of case marking occurs only in languages with either SOV or VSO as their basic clause constituent order.

6.16.4 Subject/object indexation typology

Most African languages have subject markers attached to verbs and a number of them also have object markers. Subjects markers and object markers may be obligatory and are usually termed concord or agreement markers. In fact, the term subject and object markers are unfamiliar to me. For many Benue-Congo languages, this is the case and there are examples such as the following in Ibibio, a Delta-Cross New Benue-Congo language.

76.a. (Àmì) ḿ-màá-kìt Ìmé
    1s   1sC-Past-see Ime
    'I saw Ime.'

  b. (Afo) à-màá-kìt Ìmé
    2sg   2sC-Past-see Ime
    'You saw Ime.'

c. (Ènyé) á-màá-kìt   Ìmé
   3sg   3sC-Past-see Ime
   'He/she/it saw Ime.'

77a. (Àmì) ḿ-màá-kìt   ówó kéèd
     1s   1C-Past-see person one
     'I saw one man'

b. (Àmì) ḿ-màákííd   ùwák owo
   1s   1sC-Past-see + pl many person
   'I saw many people.'

The marking on the verb indicates what in Ibibio linguistics is referred to as pluriaction. This kind of phenomenon is also found in an Upper-Cross language known as Kohumono.

6.16.5 Definiteness and referentiality

According to Creissels (2000:243), definite articles are quite common in African languages and these languages provide considerable comparative information that, in most cases, definite articles originate in demonstratives. For example in Ibibio, a New Benue-Congo language the item **ódò** means both 'that' (near the listner/hearer) and 'the'. Thus, **owo oko** is interpreted either as 'that' man or 'the man': While definite articles are said to be commonly attested to in African languages, not so indefinite articles, except by zero marking.

6.16.6 Number

Nearly all African languages make use of bound morphemes to indicate plurality, but the total lack of such markers in Igbo, one of the three major languages in Nigeria and a New Benue-Congo language is attested to.

In Africa, a three-way number set up (singular/dual/ plural) for both nouns and pronouns exists only in the central and northern branches of the Khoisan phylum. Also in African languages as number is marked both in nominal morphology and verbal morphology, where there is what Newman (1990) calls 'pluraction' by which verbs express frequentative and iterative actions in Ibibio, a Niger-Congo and Nigeria's 4th largest language, what Essien prefers to call 'pluriaction' by which plural objects are indicated on the verb also occurs.

6.16.7 Word order typology (syntax)

This has to do with the syntactic order of the phenomena subject, verb and object in a simple sentence in a language. Using Greenberg as a basis, Heine (1976) arrived at a continent-wide word-order typology of African languages, using a sample of 432 languages. He refined Greenberg's types, based on the dominant sentence order S(ubject) , O(bject) and V(erb) as follows: Type A: SVO; Type B: partly SVO; Type C: VSO; Type D: SOV. In a dominant order, a preponderance of simple sentences in a language follows the order given above. The typology may be refined, since any order may be statistically more-or-less dominant. The rest of the possible orders – VOS, OSV, OVS – are rare as primary orders.

6.16.8 Types of verbal inflection

According to Creissels (2002:238), many languages of Africa have verbal inflections which are prefixes. The proportion of languages with a predominantly prefixing inflection is higher in Africa than in most parts of the world. In addition, African languages inflection involving both segmental morphemes and tonal alternation are more than other languages, according to Creissels (2000:238).

In Kposo, the perfective vs. imperfective and positive vs. negative distinctions may rely exclusively on tonal variations of the subject marker prefixed to the verb, as in:

78. Kposo (Kwa, Niger-Congo)
    ū-dzí   'we are eating'
    úū-dzí   'we are not eating'

    ù-dzí   'we have eaten'
    ūù-dzí   'we have not eaten'

As regards the nature of the distinctions expressed through verbal inflection, three types can be distinguished and discussed:

a. In a vast majority of African languages, verbal inflection involves both subject or object markers and other types of morphemes.

b. Languages with a verbal inflection involving subject or object marker are not very common in Africa, though a number of Mande Languages (Mende, SoSo, Sonink, etc) do illustrate this.

c. Systems of verbal inflection consisting exclusively of subject and object markers are extremely, rare at world level, and among African languages, the Sara languages constitute the only case, according to Creissels (2000:239).

6.16.9 Serial verbs

Serial Verb or construction is a complex predicate made up of two or more verbs. Creissels (2000:240) has identified characteristics of this construction as given below:

i. There is a single subject for the whole sequence.

ii. Each verb may have its complement.

iii. The sequence as a whole has the behaviour of a single predicate, and not that of a construction involving distinct predicates in some dependency relation.

Creissels (2000:240) mentions the problems or difficulties of saying what serial verbs are and claims that "most of the time "there is no obvious distinction between serial verbs and verb sequences in which each verb constitutes a distinct predicate, in particular consecutive constructions, i.e. constructions in which two or more successive clauses represent successive events." For him 'true' serial constructions in African languages are not as many as found in the literature. According to him "in Africa, uncontroversial cases of serial verbs are found mainly in Kwa languages (e.g. Ewe) and in Benue-Congo languages previously classified as Eastern Kwa (e.g. Yoruba)". This is Creissels opinion which I don't necessarily share.

www.ingramcontent.com/pod-product-compliance
Lightning Source LLC
Chambersburg PA
CBHW051353290426
44108CB00015B/1992